Exploring The Noosphere: Teilhard de Chardin

The Noosphere

The Centric

The Cosmic The Human Ω The Christic

Shelli Joye

Published by the Viola Institute
Viola, California

Dedicated to Brian Swimme and Robert McDermott,
with whom I studied the cosmology of Teilhard
at the California Institute of Integral Studies;
and to my grandmother,
Lillian Roberta Lewis Faltinow,
and to my mother and father:
Lt. Col. Kenneth Edward Joye and
Jeannete Margaret Faltinow Joye,
All still dancing among the stars.

Copyright © 2018 by The Viola Institute
Printed in the United States of America

All rights reserved. No part of this publication may be reproduced, stored in a retrieval system, distributed or transmitted in any form or by any means, without prior written permission of the publisher.

Exploring the Noosphere:
Teilhard de Chardin

ISBN-13: 9781791940775

Cover painting: image by Shelli Renee Joye, acrylic & oil.

CONTENTS

Introduction 1

An Integral Approach: The New Mysticism 2

Hyperphysics: Beyond Material Science 3

Teilhard's Integral Life Experience 5

The Mystical Sense... 18

Energy: Axial and Tangential 23

A Thinking Earth: The Noosphere 25

One in Many: The Noosphere... 61

The Omega Point 64

Breaking Teilhard's "Death-Barrier" 89

    The Cross the Trinity and the Centric 91

    The Noosphere, Omega, and The Christic 93

References 97

Index... 110

Endnotes 111

*What we lack is a new domain
of psychic expansion,
and it is right in front of us,
if we would only raise our eyes.*

Teilhard de Chardin,
The Human Phenomenon (1945), 179.

Introduction

Mystics and scientists are motivated to explore the vast reaches of the cosmos, though it can be said that scientists explore the outer realities of the material universe while mystics explore the inner realities of the psychic world. Unfortunately, the two groups have seldom carefully studied one another's findings with the objective of enhancing their own understandings of cosmic reality. There has traditionally been little interest shown among the community of physical scientists to explore those maps of consciousness brought to us by generations of saints and introspective mystics.

Mystics (and saints) have rarely received sufficient training in science and technologies to model their discoveries in scientific language; similarly, scientific materialists have not often found time and interest (under the tacit threat of ridicule or censure) for an exploration of consciousness in a direct, experiential way (via introspection) to obtain the perspective required to formulate a truly effective psychophysics (hard science) of consciousness.

Pierre Teilhard de Chardin (1881–1955) was one of the rare few capable of bridging these two cultures: as a priest, mystic, and scientist, he wrote extensively and produced a model for the evolution of consciousness in the universe in scientific terms. He left behind a legacy that he hoped would forge a new mysticism, a science-based religious understanding of the dynamics of cosmos. In an optimistic note, Teilhard—a 72-year-old paleontologist, geologist, and priest—in sight of St. Helena on passage from New York, writes: "It is with irrepressible hope that I welcome the inevitable rise of this new mysticism and anticipate its equally inevitable triumph."[1]

An Integral Approach: The New Mysticism

As a supporting structure for this new mysticism, I will lay out a scientific basis for Teilhard's energy model of consciousness in the fields of electromagnetic energy, fractal mathematics, electrobiology, and psychophysics; these models are directly supported by the recently hypothesized electromagnetic field theory of consciousness put forward by the Cambridge genetic researcher, Johnjoe McFadden,[2] and Susan Pockett,[3] the New Zealand neurobiologist.

It is my contention that Teilhard's hyperphysics emerged as a product of multiple factors: a deep contemplative mystical sense combined with extensive scientific training, intense experience, and high intelligence acting together to provide a truly integral perspective. In Fig. 1 can be seen a symbolic diagram of these factors in Teilhard's unique multiperspectival consciousness.

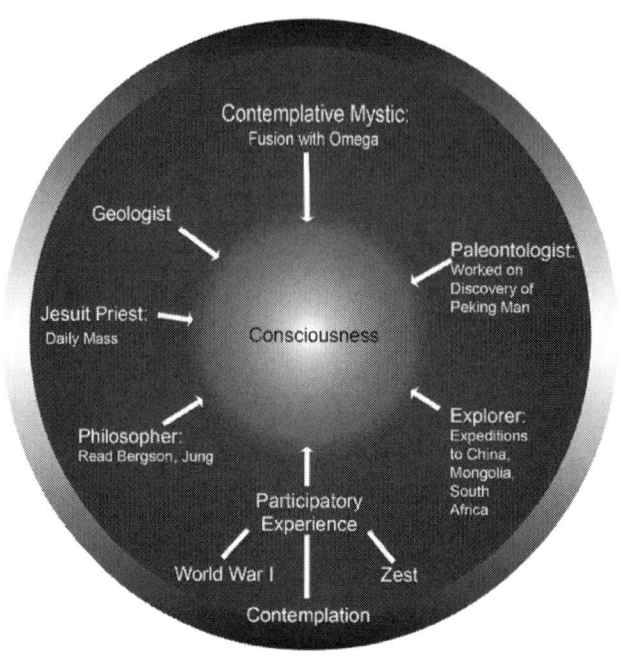

Figure 1. Teilhard's multiperspectival consciousness.

Hyperphysics: Beyond Material Science

In the first decades of the twentieth century, Marie Joseph Pierre Teilhard de Chardin,[4] a geologist, paleontologist, and priest by training, developed a model of consciousness that he referred to as "hyperphysics."[5] He conceived of this model in the context of his knowledge of physics, his keen observational skills as a geo-paleontologist, and his own specific introspective experience during a 40-year period of careful observation and consideration. In developing hyperphysics, Teilhard conducted an integral exploration of a region inclusive of and yet beyond the conceptual boundaries of physics, paleontology, or the priesthood. The objectives of this chapter are to interpret and extend Teilhard's theories of hyperphysics in general, and to discover how Teilhard's theories can be reconciled with modern physics and contemporary theories of consciousness.

In a letter to Henri de Lubac[6] dated 1934, Teilhard uses the word *hyperphysics*, describing it as a kind of metaphysics springing from the hard sciences, a metaphysics based upon science, yet "another sort of metaphysics which would really be a hyperphysics."[7] In the first sentence of the Author's Note to *The Human Phenomenon*, Teilhard states that the nature of his theories of hyperphysics is scientific, "purely and simply":

> If this book is to be properly understood it must be read not as a work on metaphysics, still less as a sort of theological essay, but purely and simply as a scientific treatise . . . only take a closer look at it, and you will see that this "hyperphysics" is not a metaphysics. [8]

It can be assumed that Teilhard, who trained in the sciences of geology and paleontology, would have been an astute observer, constantly seeking and discerning patterns in the natural world. His published professional papers led to significant recognition in the field of paleontology; when published in 1971, a collection of his scientific papers filled eleven volumes.[9] Yet, in spite of the time constraints of his dual career as priest and scientist, he was able to develop a coherent theory describing a general physics of consciousness through a long series of unpublished essays written over his lifetime. Fueled by a lifelong practice of introspective observation, often alone in the silence of nature, Teilhard elaborated his map of the dynamics of consciousness, hyperphysics.

It is likely that Teilhard never knew how his life's work in hyperphysics and the evolution of consciousness would be judged by mainstream science; the English edition of *The Phenomenon of Man* was only published in 1959, four years after his death. It was received somewhat critically both by the philosophical and the scientific community, as can be seen in this 1965 review:

> Is his proposed "hyperphysics" science?. . .There has been considerable confusion both in the United States and in Europe, where it appeared in French four years earlier, over what it is—physics, metaphysics, theology, mysticism, prophecy?[10]

Rarely has a scientist, formally trained and active in a demanding technical profession, found time and interest (under the tacit threat of ridicule or censure) to develop a theory of consciousness based upon the data of first-hand participatory experience and observation. Pierre Teilhard de Chardin was one of the few: a trained scientist, holding a doctorate in geological paleontology from the Sorbonne, who wrote regularly and extensively to produce a science-based model of the evolutionary dynamics of consciousness—an "ultraphysics of union."[11] It is a thesis of this book that for over 40 years, through direct experience, observation, and keen analysis, Teilhard laid down a foundation and a legacy that he hoped would forge a new science-based understanding of the dynamics of consciousness in an evolving cosmos.[12]

Teilhard's Integral Life Experience

It is easy to see how the region of his birth, south central France's Auvergne, instilled in Teilhard a passion for geology and nature (Fig. 2).

Figure 2. Auvergne landscape. Graphic by Romary (2006). Reprinted under the terms of a Creative Commons Attribution ShareAlike 3.0 Unported license. Image retrieved from Wikimedia Commons.

The most volcanic, mineral-rich region of France, Auvergne is also home to the largest oak forest in Europe; it was here, a few miles from the highest volcanic summit in the region, that Pierre Teilhard de Chardin was born on May 1, 1881, the fourth of 11 siblings, in his family chateau, Sarcenat.[13]

Teilhard was a direct descendent of Voltaire on his mother's side, and his father, descended from a noble family, was one of the largest landowners in the province, affording him ample free time to "build up sizeable collections of regional insects, birds, stones, and plants."[14] It was into this rich environment that Teilhard was born. At a young age, he became entranced with nature and embraced his father's passion for geology, collecting and classifying specimens. But it was his mother's influence that instilled in her young son a love of the spiritual life, and he was introduced to regular family prayer and a contemplative practice, the prayer on the Sacred Heart of Jesus. Following family tradition, Teilhard was sent to a Jesuit boarding school at the age of 11.[15]

Of all the Catholic religious congregations, the Jesuit order is especially known for its emphasis on intellectual research and scholarship, and in this environment Teilhard excelled academically. But it was here, also, that Teilhard began his daily practice of sitting for an hour in silent contemplation:

> It was at the school that he became an ascetic who voluntarily rose at dawn every day and went to sit in the chapel, often in freezing temperatures before the rest of the students awoke. He would follow a similar habit throughout his life, wherever he might be: in an Asian desert, in a prehistoric cave, or aboard a ship in rough seas.[16]

In 1899, at the age of 17, he made the decision to join the Jesuit order, and was formally accepted as a Jesuit novice, a candidate for eventual priesthood. After completing Jesuit secondary school, he was assigned abroad to teach physics and chemistry for a three-year period as part of his novitiate training. Teilhard was sent to a Jesuit-run school in Cairo, Egypt, and it was there that he first experienced the fascination of an exotic new culture, an attraction to the mystery of surrounding antiquities, and most of all, perhaps, the experience of profound silence in the vastness of a desert.[17]

> It was immediately after I had experienced such sense of wonder in Egypt that there gradually grew in me, as a *presence* much more than as an abstract notion, the consciousness of a deep-running, ontological, total Current which embraced the whole

Universe in which I moved; and this consciousness continued to grow until it filled the whole horizon of my inner being.[18]

Upon returning from Egypt in 1909, Teilhard spent several years studying philosophy and theology at a Jesuit center in Hastings, a coastal town 60 miles southeast of London. It was during this time that he carefully read and reread *Creative Evolution*, a recently published work by the popular French philosopher Henri Bergson (1859–1941), a book the Vatican would soon place on its Index of Forbidden Books.[19] Previously, Teilhard had uncritically accepted the then-held theory on the *fixity* of species, and though he knew of Darwin's theories, they had seemed to him only an interesting hypothesis—one certainly suspect in the eyes of his Jesuit community. But after a careful reading of Bergson's *Creative Evolution*, Teilhard found himself suddenly a "convinced evolutionist," in strong agreement with Bergson's arguments for evolution even as he disagreed with Bergson's vision of a "pre-existing and obdurate matter" being operated upon by a life-force energy, which Bergson named *élan vital*. Teilhard himself felt that Bergson's life-force was never to be found remote from matter, but from inception was at the very heart of matter.[20]

The dynamics of evolution, according to Bergson, is powered by a "vital" force of energy animating not only life but the unfolding of the cosmos, and this force fundamentally connects consciousness and body. This idea stood in radical contrast to the widely accepted belief in the *dualism* of matter and consciousness set forth by the seventeenth-century philosopher-scientist René Descartes.[21]

The young Teilhard was especially impressed with Bergson's emphasis on the importance of *intuition* and *immediate experience*, as these were Teilhard's own tools, developed and honed during his daily contemplative practices.

Through immediate experience, he was able to observe directly the structure and dynamics of his own inner space, his own complexity-consciousness in process; he says that this led to "a new intuition that totally alters the physiognomy of the universe in which we move, in other words, in an awakening."[22] Near the end of his life, Teilhard comments on the early influence of Bergson's book:

> I can remember very clearly the avidity with which, at that time, I read Bergson's *Creative Evolution* . . . I can now see quite clearly that the effect that brilliant book had upon me was to provide fuel at just the right moment . . . for a fire that was already consuming my heart and mind. And that fire had been kindled.[23]

The effect of Bergson's ideas upon Teilhard's worldview was significant indeed. In 1930, Teilhard wrote of Bergson in a letter to his close friend Leontine Zanta (the first French woman to receive a doctorate in philosophy): "I pray for that admirable man and venerate him as a kind of saint."[24] According to Teilhard's biographer Ursula King, after reading *Creative Evolution*,

> The magic word "evolution" haunted his thoughts "like a tune"; it was to him "like an unsatisfied hunger, like a promise held out to me, like a summons to be answered." Evolution was vital. It was the necessary condition of all further scientific thought.[25]

In 1912, Teilhard began formal graduate studies in geology and paleontology, eventually leading to his doctorate; as a student, he also began working at the Museum of Natural History in Paris. In 1914 he was called up for service by the French Army and quickly trained as a medical orderly.[26] After serving for some time behind the lines, he volunteered to be

8

reassigned to the western front as a stretcher bearer rather than as an army chaplain, and on January 22, 1915, he was assigned to a regiment of Moroccan light infantry, where "on arrival Teilhard made himself look like an Arab by exchanging his field-service blue for the khaki colors of the African troops, and his kepi for a red fez."[27]

It was here, alongside members of this regiment of Algerian tribesmen, that Teilhard served for over three years in the trenches of the front lines. Teilhard was the only Christian in his regiment, but by the end of the war he was referred to affectionately by the North African Muslim soldiers he lived with in the trenches as *"Sidi Marabout,"* an acknowledgement of his spiritual power as a man closely bound to God, protected from all injuries by divine grace."[28] After the war, at the request of his war-time regiment, Teilhard was awarded the French Legion of Honour for bravery.[29] His citation reads:

> An outstanding stretcher-bearer, who during four years of active service was in every battle and engagement the regiment took part in, applying to remain in the ranks in order that he might be with the men whose dangers and hardships he constantly shared.[30]

Teilhard thus witnessed first-hand, for a protracted period of his life, the enormous suffering and destruction of human life that was the characteristic brutality of war. Such experience was in sharp contrast to his academic life.

It was in Belgium that Teilhard experienced the true horror of World War I. When they arrived at Ypres, the troops found a town that had just been burned down. Hundreds of soldiers lay on the ground, dead or dying—and after the Germans were through with their conventional weapons strike, they attacked their enemy with poison gas.[31]

Yet the young scholar/priest seemed to display no fear, at least to his closest colleagues. One of his fellow soldiers at the time, Max Bégoüen, wrote the following description of an event he witnessed on the Belgian front in 1915:

> The North African sharpshooters of his regiment thought he was protected by his *baraka* (an Arabic word meaning "spiritual stature" or "supernatural quality"). The curtain of machine gun fire and the hail of bombardments both seemed to pass him by. During the attacks of September 2 at Artois, my brother was wounded, and, as he wandered on the battlefield, he saw a single stretcher bearer rising up in front of him, and he, for it was Teilhard, accomplished his mission quite imperturbably under terrible ire . . . "I thought I had seen the appearance of a messenger from God."
>
> I once asked Father Teilhard, "What do you do to keep this sense of calm during battle? It looks as if you do not see the danger and that fear does not touch you."
>
> He answered, with that serious but friendly smile which gave such a human warmth to his words, "If I am killed, I shall just change my state, that's all."[32]

For four years he served as an unarmed stretcher-bearer at Verdun, until 1917, and thereafter in the front trenches of Château-Thierry in 1918, participating in action of such great ferocity that it took the lives of over nine million of his fellow soldiers. The accounts of his disregard of his own safety in order to rescue the wounded of all nationalities eventually led to his being awarded the Chevalier de la Legion d'Honneur in 1921 for bravery in action.

We can only imagine the experiences this young man must have lived through—the sounds, the sights, the deprivations of weather and humanity—yet out of the intensity of this existential life "on the Front," Teilhard began to experience a new form of consciousness not only in his own mind but as a "quasi-collective" participatory functioning flux becoming "fully conscious," as he describes in a letter written at the front in 1917:

> I'm still in the same quiet billets. Our future continues to be pretty vague, both as to when and what it will be. What the future imposes on our present existence is not exactly a feeling of depression; it's rather a sort of seriousness, of detachment, of a broadening, too, of outlook. ... but it leads also to a sort of higher joy, ... I'd call it "Nostalgia for the Front." The reasons, I believe, come down to this; the front cannot but attract us because it is, in one way, the extreme boundary between what one is already aware of, and what is still in process of formation. Not only does one see there things that you experience nowhere else, but *one also sees emerge from within one an underlying stream of clarity, energy, and freedom that is to be found hardly anywhere else in ordinary life - and the new form that the soul then takes on is that of the individual living the quasi-collective life of all* men, fulfilling a function far higher than that of the individual, and becoming fully conscious of this new state. .... This exaltation is accompanied by a certain pain. Nevertheless it is indeed an exaltation. And that's why one likes the front in spite of everything, and misses it.[33]

During this time and under these conditions he began to experience, observe, and ultimately write about his own direct awareness of nonordinary states of consciousness. For example, it was at the front that he began to directly perceive, for the first time, a sense of collective consciousness over and above his own. In his 1917 essay "Nostalgia for the Front," Teilhard asks, "Is it not ridiculous to be so drawn into the magnetic field of the war ... more than ever the Front casts its spell over me. . . . What is it, then, that I myself have seen at the front?"[34] He answers himself by saying, "it is above all something more, something more subtle and more substantial, I might define it as a superhuman state to which the soul is borne." Having left the front lines, he experiences a feeling of loss: "I have the feeling of having lost a soul, a soul greater than my own, which lives in the trenches and which I have left behind."[35]

When trying to understand the impact of these experiences on the young Teilhard, it is worthwhile to consider that at Verdun, where Teilhard served during one of the most protracted battles of the war, the single battle continued for over nine months and the human losses approached apocalyptic proportions:

> A French estimate that is probably not excessive places the total French and German losses on the Verdun battlefield at 420,000 dead, and 800,000 gassed or wounded; nearly a million and a quarter in all.[36]

It was at Verdun on October 14, 1916—the night before the attack on Fort Douaumont—that Teilhard experienced an extraordinary vision, which he recounted afterwards in the short essay "Christ in Matter."[37] Here, in the visual imagery alone, one can only imagine that Teilhard was experiencing a major psychotropic vision, perhaps brought on by fatigue, synesthesia from the constant bombardment, or from the stress of being continually at the front on the eve of a major offensive attack.

The Powerful Vision

The imagery of Teilhard's vision is so intense and specific here that one even wonders if he might have ingested ergot-infected rye bread (ergot mold on rye bread has been reported to induce LSD-like symptoms; in 1951, an entire French village became infected with the ergot alkaloid and experienced hallucinations).[38] Here is Teilhard's description of this pivotal, altered-state experience that occurred in an abandoned chapel, at night, during the Battle of Verdun:

> Suppose, I thought, that Christ should deign to appear here, in the flesh, before my very eyes—what would he look like? Most important of all, in what way would he fit himself into Matter and so be sensibly apprehended? . .Meanwhile, my eyes had unconsciously come to rest on a picture that represented Christ with his Heart offered to men. This picture was hanging in front of me, on the wall of a church into which I had gone to pray . . . I was still looking at the picture when the vision began. (Indeed, I cannot be certain exactly when it began, because it had already reached a certain pitch of intensity when I became aware of it.) All I know is that as I let my eyes roam over the outlines of the picture, I suddenly realized that they *were melting*. They were melting, but in a very special way that I find it difficult to describe.
>
> If I relaxed my visual concentration, the whole of Christ's outline, the folds of his robe, the bloom of his skin, merged (though without disappearing) into all the rest . . . the edge which divided Christ from the surrounding World was changing into a layer of vibration in which all distinct delimitation was lost . . . I noticed that the vibrant atmosphere which formed a halo around Christ was not confined to a narrow strip encircling him, but radiated into Infinity. From time to time what seemed to be trails of phosphorescence streamed across it, in which could be seen a continuous pulsing surge which reached out to the furthest spheres of matter— forming a sort of crimson ganglion, or nervous network, running across every substance. *The whole Universe was vibrating.* . . . It was thus that the light and the colours of all the beauties we know shone,

with an inexpressible iridescence . . . these countless modifications followed one another in succession, were transformed, melted into one another in a harmony that was utterly satisfying to me . . . I was completely at a loss. *I found it impossible to decipher.* . . . All I know is that, since that occasion, I believe I have seen a hint of it once, and that was in the eyes of a dying soldier.[39]

Decades later, Teilhard refers to this epiphanic experience, this "particular interior event" of 40 years prior.[40] He describes how it has been that since this early revelation, he has had "the capacity to see two fundamental psychic movements or currents," which, when he first perceived them in his 1916 epiphany, "reacted endlessly upon one another in a flash of extraordinary brilliance, releasing . . . a light so intense that it transfigured for me the very depths of the World."[41] In his final essay, completed a month before his death, Teilhard stresses the *objective validity* of this initial evidence that had led directly to his new understanding of consciousness and the universe, evidence which had presented itself to him experientially in 1916:

> What follows is not a mere speculative dissertation in which the main lines of some long-matured and cleverly constructed system are set out. It constitutes the evidence brought to bear, with complete objectivity, *upon a particular interior event, upon a particular personal experience.* . . . Today, after forty years of continuous thought, it is still exactly the same fundamental vision that I feel I must present, and enable others to share in its matured form—for the last time.[42]

It is this subsequent "forty years of continuous thought" that makes the uniqueness of his observations, expressed in his essays, so significant for the development of consciousness studies. Four sides of Teilhard's nature reinforced one another, integrally it would seem: scientific training, mystical vision, exceptional intelligence, and a passionate enthusiasm for discovery and understanding. While he was formally a scientist, highly trained and experienced in the observation, collection, classification, and written interpretation of geological and anthropological data, he was also a Jesuit priest, deeply immersed in observing the internal phenomena of spirit during his daily contemplative period. His was a quest to bring scientific reasoning and understanding to bear upon a direct vision, one that has been described by his biographer as

> a powerful vision linked to experiences of a deeply mystical, or what might be called pan-entheistic, character although he often simply called them "pantheistic." These experiences occurred over many years.[43]

Throughout his writing, one encounters passages that can only be seen to refer directly to a personal experience of a sort of perception that he himself categorized as pantheism and mystical vision (which, along with his fascination with evolution, caused him enduring conflict with more conservative forces in the Vatican). Teilhard states that his perception, "as experience shows, is indeed the result . . . of a mystic absorbed in divine contemplation."[44] Elsewhere Teilhard regards this special psychic perception as a natural ability, but one that requires practice and cultivation in order to catalyze the necessary change of state in consciousness:

> This perception of a natural psychic unity higher than our "souls" requires, as I know from experience, a special quality and training in the observer. . . once we manage to affect this change of viewpoint then the earth, our little human earth, is draped in a splendor. Floating above the biosphere, whose layers no doubt

15

gradually merge into it, the world of thought, the noosphere, begins to let its crown shine. The noosphere![45]

Teilhard's contemplative, mystical interests began at an early age; then, he searched to discern some "Absolute" in his experience of prayer with his large Catholic family, described here in "My Universe," which was written on the battlefield of the Marne, three weeks after the beginning of a major attack by the Germans:

> However far back I go into my memories (even before the age of ten) I can distinguish in myself the presence of a strictly dominating passion: the passion for the Absolute. At that age, of course, I did not so describe the urgent concern I felt; but today I can put a name to it without any possible hesitation. Ever since my childhood, the need to lay hold of "some Absolute" in everything was the axis of my inner life.[46]

During 1926 and 1927 Teilhard wrote *The Divine Milieu* while working in China, where he had effectively been banished by the Jesuit authorities; it is in the middle of this essay that he describes what can be only understood as a personal experience of deep contemplation in which, through a process of increasing centro-complexity, he began to travel consciously toward an encounter with a heretofore unimagined depth of inner being:

> And so, for the first time in my life perhaps (although I am supposed to meditate every day!), I took the lamp and, leaving the zone of everyday occupations and relationships where everything seems clear, I went down into my inmost self, to the deep abyss whence I feel dimly that my power of action emanates. But as I moved further and further away from the conventional certainties by which social life

is superficially illuminated, I became aware that I was losing contact with myself. At each step of the descent a new person was disclosed within me of whose name I was no longer sure, and who no longer obeyed me. And when I had to stop my exploration because the path faded from beneath my steps, I found a bottomless abyss at my feet, and out of it came—arising I know not from where—the current which I dare to call *my* life. What science will ever be able to reveal to man the origin, nature and character of that conscious power. . .? Stirred by my discovery, I then wanted to return to the light of day and forget the disturbing enigma in the comfortable surroundings of familiar things.[47]

In the development of Teilhard's mystical sense, the possibility cannot be ruled out that Teilhard in midlife had the occasion to experience consciousness-expanding drugs, which would have provided new material for development of his theories of consciousness. On an ocean passage from France to China in 1926, Teilhard had befriended a French couple with a homestead in East Africa: Henry de Monfried and his wife, Armgart.[48] Monfried has been variously described as "a pirate, a smuggler, and an arms dealer."[49] Nevertheless the three immediately developed strong bonds that lasted for decades, and Teilhard would often visit them in their East African home during his many voyages between Asia and France. As one of Teilhard's biographers commented:

> Teilhard was so attracted to this couple that, still aboard the *Angkor*, he confessed to Armgart, "I have full faith in Henry, in what he says about himself; but even more truly, I love you, you and him."[50]

On a return voyage from China three years later, Teilhard stopped in East Africa to join Henry and Armgart for a visit, with apparently no reservations at all concerning the use of opium: according to Teilhard's biographer, Jacques Arnould, "Teilhard brought Monfried opium from China—'for his personal use.'"[51] On another occasion, Teilhard saved Monfried from arrest by local authorities in China when Monfried was trying to pick up a shipment of hashish in Chinese Turkistan.[52] It should be noted that the use of hashish and opium was widespread in China during this time, and we can assume that the European enclave of intellectuals and artists in Peking in the "roaring 20s" may likely have experimented with psychotropics such as hashish and opium, particularly as the practice was not illegal during Teilhard's years in Peking:

> Ma Fuxiang [a Chinese warlord in the early 20th century] officially prohibited opium and made it illegal in Ningxia [included Peking], but the Guominjun reversed his policy; by 1933, people from every level of society were using the drug.[53]

In such an environment, during his decade long friendship with the American artist Lucile Swan, it is not beyond consideration that Teilhard may have experienced the psychotropic effects of hashish and/or opium, which would have only provided rich psychic material for self-observation and development of his ideas concerning a hyperphysics of consciousness, noosphere, and the Omega point.

The Mystical Sense

Our thesis holds that over his lifetime, Teilhard's mystical sense aligned with his rigorous scientifically trained skill in observation as a geologist and paleontologist; when coupled with his Jesuit training in logic, clarity, and expressive writing, this combination gifted him with the ability to record his ideas prolifically. In addition to *11* volumes of scientific publications published during his lifetime, there now exist *13* volumes of speculative philosophy, all published after his death.[54] In 1951 he wrote a short essay entitled "Some Notes on the Mystical Sense: An Attempt at Clarification," which begins with the following sentences:

> The mystical sense is essentially a feeling for, a presentiment of, the total and final unity of the world, beyond its present sensibly apprehended multiplicity: it is a cosmic sense of "oneness." It enables us to become one with all by co-extension "with the sphere": that is to say, by suppression of all internal and external determinants, to come together with a sort of common stuff which *underlies* the variety of concrete beings. It is access to Aldous Huxley's "common ground."[55]

It is clear that Teilhard as geologist/paleontologist was in an ideal position for observing, documenting, and interpreting the direct experiences of the inner life of Teilhard the contemplative priest. This integral configuration underlies the development of his "hyperphysics," his "physics of centration."[56]

After World War II, having just spent six years in relative isolation under the Japanese occupation, Teilhard gave a lecture at the French Embassy in Peking, in which he talked about the "growing importance with which leading thinkers of all denominations are beginning to attach to the phenomenon of mysticism."[57] He went on to describe mysticism in the perception of the Omega point:

> Let us suppose that from this universal centre, this Omega point, there constantly emanate radiations hitherto only perceptible to those persons whom we call "mystics." Let us further imagine that, as the sensibility or response to mysticism of the human race increases with planetisation, the awareness of

Omega becomes so widespread as to warm the earth psychically.[58]

That Teilhard's understanding grew over the arc of his lifetime is evident in essays striving to express his vision, those written beginning in World War I and continuing until his death in 1955. In all of his essays, his motivated energy to clearly express the framework of his understanding in words can be detected:

> It seems to me that a whole lifetime of continual hard work would be as nothing to me, if only I could, just for one moment, give a true picture of what I see.[59]

In 1922 Teilhard was awarded his doctorate, defending his thesis on mammals of the Lower Eocene (56 to 33.9 million years ago) in France.[60] According to a biographer, "The board of examiners had no hesitation in conferring on him the title of doctor, with distinction."[61] In that same year, the British psychologist Conway Lloyd Morgan (1852–1936) presented a series of radical new ideas at speaker at the Gifford Lectures, in which he extended the ideas of Henri Bergson.[62] Morgan described how an observed increase of complexity in the evolutionary process often results in discontinuous leaps with the past, rather than through the more gradual, steady process that had been predicted by the theory of Darwinian natural selection.[63] Lloyd Morgan's theory can be seen as a precursor to an expression of the dynamics of complexity-consciousness in Teilhard's own hyperphysics. The direct effect of centro-complexification, according to Teilhard, catalyzes transformation in the organization and functioning of consciousness, causing a phase shift, as when water crystallizes into ice or transforms into steam. It is this principle of centro-complexity that initiates and drives this catalysis.

Unfortunately, essays such as "Centrology," which develops the theory of centro-complexity in detail, were never published in Teilhard's lifetime. Conservative elements in the Catholic hierarchy made it difficult if not impossible for him to publish much of his work, in great part because the Church had not yet reconciled the science of evolution with doctrinal Catholicism, and Teilhard's essays and lectures soared unchecked on a wave of evolutionary ideas.

Though Teilhard was forbidden to teach, lecture, or publish outside of a narrow range of scientific material, his strictly scientific publications fill 11 volumes, indicating the extent of his output and reflecting his professional stature as a world-class paleontologist. Teilhard's books and essays on speculative philosophy and the evolution of consciousness, on the other hand, though only published posthumously between 1955 and 1976, fill another 13 volumes.[64]

Certainly, being forbidden to publish had its effect on Teilhard. To keep him out of Paris, where the Church saw his ideas as attracting too much enthusiasm among young seminarians, he was virtually banished from Paris and placed on assignment in China early in his career, and then banished again to America after the war, near the end of his life.[65] These challenges (some might say affronts) to the expression of his richest ideas, coupled perhaps with the first-hand horror and suffering he experienced during two world wars, must have taken a toll on his emotional side, and must surely have contributed to his frequent bouts of despondence and depression. Pierre Leroy, his friend and colleague throughout their years of confinement in Peking who, at 20 years Teilhard's junior, first met him in 1928 in Paris, writes of Teilhard's bouts of depression:

> Many have rightly been struck by Pere Teilhard's great optimism. He was indeed an optimist, in his

attribution to the universe of a sense of direction in spite of the existence of evil and in spite of appearances... but how often in intimate conversation have I found him depressed and with almost no heart to carry on.... During that period he was at times prostrated by fits of weeping, and he appeared to be on the verge of despair.... Six years thus went by in the dispiriting atmosphere of China occupied by the Japanese and cut off from the rest of the world.[66]

Yet when Teilhard was finally able to leave China at war's end, he wrote, during the sea passage on his return to France: "These seven years have made me quite grey, but they have toughened me—not hardened me, I hope—interiorly."[67] He retained the passion and motivation to write extensively, particularly in his later years, and he continued the development of his observations and conclusions regarding consciousness and the dynamics of energy in an evolving universe. He himself would likely have characterized the gift of this persevering energy with the term "zest," which he defines it here a 1950 essay:

> By "zest for living" or "zest for life," I mean here, to put it very approximately, that spiritual disposition, at once intellectual and affective, in virtue of which life, the world, and action seem to us, on the whole, luminous—interesting—appetizing.[68]

It is almost as if the restriction placed upon him by the Church against publication gave him free rein to explore his ideas in essays that were freely distributed among his closest friends and many acquaintances. In spite of the censorship of the Church, many unofficial copies of his writings were made, and most have been published in posthumous collections.[69] One of his most profound essays, "Centrology: An Essay in a

Dialectic of Union," discussed in detail later in this chapter, was written in his period of isolation in Peking during Japanese wartime occupation.[70] Soon after emerging from his seclusion in China, Teilhard was deeply disappointed when the Vatican forbade him to publish what he considered to be his major work, *The Human Phenomenon*, while simultaneously refusing him permission to accept the offer of a prestigious teaching chair. Yet in spite of such opposition to his visionary understanding of the energy of consciousness, it has been noted that "he wrote *more* religious and philosophical essays in the years 1946–1955 than during any other period of his life—his bibliography lists over ninety titles for this time."[71]

Energy: Axial and Tangential

Energy is the central element in Teilhard's technical modeling of the cosmos. He says that while "in metaphysics the notion of being can be defined with a precision that is geometric," things are not so clear in physics, where the notion of energy is "still open to all sorts of possible corrections or improvements."[72] Teilhard's essays on the energy of consciousness, spanning four decades, systematically introduce a coherent range of such corrections and improvements. In the last page of his essay, "Activation of Energy," Teilhard states, "there are two different energies one axial, increasing, and irreversible, and the other peripheral or tangential, constant, and reversible: and these two energies are linked together in 'arrangement.'"[73] Thus Teilhard's hyperphysics posits two modes, domains, or dimensions of energy, not only of a *tangential component* of energy that operates within space–time dimensions, and which is measured and explored by modern physics, but also a *radial* or *axial component* of energy. It is this axial energy that provides the direct link with the

23

center Teilhard termed Omega, which guides, informs, and maintains the evolutionary process throughout the space–time cosmos.[74] He describes this radial component of energy as "a new dimensional zone" that brings with it "new properties," and he describes how increasing centration along the radial component leads to increasing states of "complexity-consciousness."[75] As Teilhard says here:

> Science in its present reconstructions of the world fails to grasp an essential factor, or, to be more exact, an entire dimension of the universe ... all we need to do is to take the inside of things into account at the same time as the outside.[76]

Energy, for Teilhard, is not simply regarded as a mathematical abstraction. He views energy as the matrix of consciousness, the driver of evolution, and as a living, communicating radiation or flux. For Teilhard, energy is "a true 'transcosmic' radiation for which the organisms ... would seem to be precisely the naturally provided receivers."[77]

Teilhard is critical of the one-dimensional approach to energy taken by contemporary research. He asks, "What is the relationship between this interior energy ... and the goddess of energy worshipped by physicists?"[78] His answer is that there are two fundamental categories or modes of energy, and implies that physicists deal with but one mode. In his own words, "We still persist in regarding the physical as constituting the 'true' phenomenon in the universe, and the psychic as a sort of epiphenomenon."[79]

He also describes these two components of energy in physical and the psychic terms: "*physical energy* being no more than *materialized psychic energy*,"[80] but he is not able to posit a mathematical or physical relationship between these two dimensions other than to express the hope that "there must surely be some hidden relationship which links them together in their development."[81]

A Thinking Earth: The Noosphere

Despite clerical resistance to his ideas, Teilhard continued to be fascinated by what he saw as the emerging evolution of a collective human consciousness upon the planet Earth: the emergence of a "thinking Earth," a phenomenon that he had directly intuited in his intense experiences at the war front in 1917. He continued his dual work in the fields of paleontology and speculative philosophy; for example, in January 1923 he finished an essay, "Pantheism and Christianity," only to publish "Paleontology and the Appearance of Man" two months later.[82]

Those powerful wartime experiences, however, led Teilhard to the perception of an emerging planetary consciousness, which he termed the *noosphere*[83]; after his death, it was conceptualized as *"an ultimate and inevitable sphere of evolution . . . a scientific approach with a bridge to religion."*[84]

During the war, Teilhard had given the name "The Great Monad" to his conception and experience of an emerging consciousness.[85] But by 1920, during his doctoral studies, he was using the term "Anthroposphere" in referring to this thinking sphere of the planet.[86] In Paris in 1921, drawn together by similar interests, Édouard Le Roy (1870–1954) and Teilhard de Chardin met and became friends. A mathematician and philosopher by training, Le Roy immediately found in Teilhard an intellectual equal, and the two began a lifetime relationship, leading with the year to the exploration of a new concept, the noosphere.[87] Le Roy had studied with Henri Bergson and had become known as his protégé; subsequently, he had been appointed successor to Bergson at the College de France.[88]

Though 10 years Teilhard's senior, the two soon began a series of informal weekly discussions:

> Punctually, at 8:30 p.m., on Wednesday evenings Teilhard would call at Le Roy's apartment in the Rue Cassette, and it was not long before the two men were thinking and speaking with a single mind.[89]

Though Le Roy was a decade older than Teilhard, their relationship appears to have been considerably more than simple mentorship. Teilhard wrote,

> I loved him like a father, and owed him a very great debt . . . he gave me confidence, enlarged my mind, and served as a spokesman for my ideas, then taking shape, on "hominization" and the "noosphere."[90]

Over their many months of frequent discussion, the two grew so close in their philosophical thought that Le Roy would later say in one of his books:

> I have so often and for so long talked over with Pere Teilhard the views expressed here that neither of us can any longer pick out his own contribution.[91]

Their meetings soon included a mutual acquaintance, the brilliant writer Vladimir Ivanovich Vernadsky (1863–1945), a distinguished Russian geologist from St. Petersburg who eventually founded the field known as biogeochemistry. Vernadsky popularized his term "the biosphere" in a series of lectures at the Sorbonne from 1922–1923, and Le Roy and Teilhard were frequent attendees.[92]

Vernadsky viewed the phenomenon of life as a natural and integral part of the cosmos, and not merely some epiphenomenon. Accordingly, he professed that universal physical laws, discovered by science over a wide range of seemingly disparate fields, would eventually find continuation with fundamental principles that are the ground of life.[93]

Although he is not widely acknowledged in the West, Vernadsky was the first to recognize the importance of life as a geological force, an idea that predates the more recent Gaia hypothesis:

> James E. Lovelock, the British inventor and the other major scientific contributor to the concept of an integrated biosphere in this century, remained unaware of Vernadsky's work until well after Lovelock framed his own Gaia hypothesis. Whereas Vernadsky's work emphasized life as a geological force, Lovelock has shown that earth has a physiology: the temperature, alkalinity, acidity, and reactive gases are modulated by life.[94]

Teilhard left Paris for China on April 6, 1923, booking inexpensive shipping routes that gave him opportunity to spend time exploring the Suez, Ceylon, Sumatra, Saigon, and Hong Kong before arriving in Shanghai. During his time at sea, he had ample hours to think about and to observe the biosphere:

> Teilhard spent his time aboard ship reading, writing, and observing nature. He liked to look at the stars at night—so clear and bright when seen from a ship far from the intruding lights of terra firma—and by day observe the state of the ocean, calm at times and stormy at others.[95]

On May 6, 1923, barely a month after departing from Marseille, Teilhard completed the essay that would later be titled "Hominization," seting forth his first extended exploration of the "Noosphere" concept, which may be considered an outgrowth of recent discussions with Vernadsky and Le Roy in Paris."[96] In the essay, Teilhard begins by making a subtle shift from the usual Cartesian linear approach to paleontological classification toward a more spherical, three-dimensional metaphysical geometry: "We begin to understand that the most natural division of the elements of the earth would be by zones, by circles, by *spheres*."[97] In the last half of the essay, Teilhard develops his understanding of the "Noosphere" concept, and in one section, "The Psychic Essence of Evolution," Teilhard says:

> It has appeared as a possible element in a sort of higher organism which might form itself . . .or else something (someone) exists, in which each element gradually finds, by reunion with the whole, the completion of all the savable elements that have been formed in its individuality.[98]

In this "reunion with the whole" can be seen a foreshadowing of the main theme of one of his final essays, written thirty-two years later: "The Death-Barrier and Co-Reflection," in which he describes a process in which each individual human, at least the "savable elements," transcend the physical death barrier to merge with the Noosphere due to "the principles of the conservation of consciousness . . .conceived as the luminous attainment of *a new psychological stage*."[99]

Barely a week before his own death, Teilhard concludes his "breaking the death-barrier" essay with the statement that "the interior equilibrium of what we have called the Noosphere requires the presence *perceived by individuals* of a higher pole or centre that directs, sustains and assembles the whole sheaf of our efforts."[100] The emphasis that Teilhard places on the words "perceived by individuals" can be seen here to underscore the experiential, participatory dimension of his quest to explore and understand the dynamics of the planet Earth, considering it—certainly from Vernadsky's biospheric view—as an evolving organism at every level.

But in 1924, thirty-two years before his final essay, Teilhard found himself in a state of withdrawal as he arrived in China, a somewhat banished intellectual from Paris. Commenting about Teilhard's state of mind at that time, a friend wrote, "His friends noticed that he seemed to be abstracted and withdrawn."[101] Teilhard himself writes, shortly after his arrival in China, "I feel very much as though I had reached the limit of my powers: I seem somehow unable to keep things in my mind. I have the continual feeling that as far as my own life goes, the day is drawing to a close."[102]

Arriving in the Chinese city of Tientsin (today's industrial port city of Tianjin), he joined the French "Paleontological Mission in China" founded by his fellow priest Fr. Licent (whom Teilhard soon discovered to be the sole other member of the "Paleontological Mission"). After a two-week stay in Tientsin, he found himself departing on his first expedition into upper Mongolia and the mountainous Ordos desert with his fellow priest, Licent, who himself had been exploring Mongolia for the past nine years. They were travelling to an area where Licent had discovered fossil deposit sites; he had previously shipped specimens from the Tertiary Period (65 million to 2.6 million years ago) to Teilhard in Paris.

The two priests traveled and camped for over a year in the vast silence of Mongolia. Even today, Inner Mongolia, Gansu, and Xinjiang are considered isolated areas of China. In an early 1924 letter Teilhard writes, "I looked over the steppes where gazelles still run about as they did in the Tertiary period, or visited the yurts where the Mongols still live as they lived a thousand years ago."[103]

It was here, during this extended period of solitude in the Mongolian high desert plains, on some silent bright day or crystalline night under the canopy of stars, that Teilhard experienced a new realization, a new communion with God and the universe. If we read carefully, we can even pick out expressions of these particular moments as they are recorded in *The Divine Milieu* (1927), when a young priest begins to establish this connection consciously—becoming one with the energies of the divine being in the surrounding landscape:

> On some given day a man suddenly becomes conscious that he is alive to a particular perception of the divine spread everywhere about him. . . . It began with a particular and unique resonance which swelled each harmony, with a diffused radiance . . . And then, contrary to all expectation and all probability, I began to feel what was ineffably common to all things. The unity communicated itself to me by giving me the gift of grasping it. I had in fact acquired a new sense, *the sense of a new quality or of a new dimension.* Deeper still: a transformation had taken place for me in *the very perception of being.*[104]

The result of this transformation was a new level of written communication and communion, as his friend Pierre Leroy recounts: "It was during this expedition, in the stillness of the vast solitude of the Ordos desert, that one Easter Sunday he finished the mystical and philosophical poem, *Mass upon the altar of the World.*"

As to how Teilhard attained to this "new sense in the very perception of being" or precisely what occurred to establish the connection to this "hidden power stirring in the heart of matter, glowing centre," he does not give a clue; however, he personalizes it and gives it a name, "the *divine milieu*," characterizing it as a sound, a single note, an "ineffably simple vibration":

> Just as, at the center of the divine *milieu*, all the sounds of created being are fused, without being confused, *in a single note* which dominates and sustains them (that seraphic note, no doubt, which

bewitched St. Francis), so all the powers of the soul begin to resound in response to its call; and these multiple tones, in their turn, compose themselves into a single, *ineffably simple vibration* in which all the spiritual nuances . . . shine forth . . . inexpressible and unique.[105]

Teilhard assures us that this new sense arises from a profound interior vision: "One thing at least appears certain, that God never reveals himself to us from outside, by intrusion, but from within, by stimulation, elevation and enrichment of the human psychic current."[106]

In 1927, under the heading "The Growth of the Divine Milieu," he writes:

> Let us therefore concentrate upon a better understanding *of the process by which the holy presence is born and grows within us.* In order to foster its progress more intelligently let us observe the birth and growth of the divine milieu, first in ourselves and then in the world that begins with us.[107]

Being a Catholic priest, Teilhard easily associated the cosmic Christ with the Omega Point, and saw this confluence as being a harmonious solution to the problem of bringing his vision into alignment with his faith (and with his employer, the Vatican, who nevertheless at that time censored his speculative essays in toto). In a 1945 essay Teilhard writes, "Just suppose that we identify the cosmic Christ of faith with the Omega Point of science: then everything in our outlook is clarified and broadened, and falls into harmony."[108]

In 1955, almost thirty years after his early experiences of the *Milieu* in the trenches at Verdun and in the vast Mongolian desert—and just two weeks before his death on an Easter Sunday in New York—Teilhard completed "The Christic."[109] Only twenty pages long, this final essay describes his mature vision, integrating science and religion, and recapturing his earlier first experiences of the psychic movements or currents.

In the first section of the essay, "The Amorization of the Universe," we find a summary of Teilhard's many years of experiencing "the two fundamental psychic movements or currents." These two fundamental currents can be seen to reflect his distinct vision of energy as having two mutually perpendicular components (like the Cross) or movements: a tangential flow in space and time that fills the cosmos with the creative electrical radiance of resonant matter, and a second current, a magnetic radial inflow of energy resonance—of spirit returning to the source, the process of centration, of noogenesis, of Christification leading toward Omega.

"On the one side," says Teilhard, is "the irresistible convergence of my individual thought with every other thinking being on earth" and "a flux, at once physical and psychic."[110] This is the tangential seen here as the very flux of collective thought on the planet Earth, an experience of the matrix-like web of human consciousness active in the biosphere.

> And on the other side . . . a centration of my own small ego . . . a sort of Other who could be even more I than I am myself . . . a Presence so intimate that it could not satisfy itself or satisfy me, without being by nature universal. [111]

Here is expressed the magnetically radial component of consciousness, the energy of centration pulling inwardly toward a center which, perhaps beyond the event horizon of time-space, is also the universal Center, the Omega, the ultimate personalization of human cosmogenesis, fully personalized and identified by Teilhard the Catholic priest as "the Christic."

Upon returning to Paris, after having spent 18 months on his extended expedition to Mongolia, Teilhard resumed teaching classes at the Institut Catholique, from which he had taken a leave of absence.[112]

Teilhard gave four lectures on evolution during the winter months of 1925; and at the same time continued to develop his theory of the noosphere—a kind of cosmic envelope created by the reflection of the mind. The word was his own invention—it had come to him during the war—but the word and the idea were both adopted later by Le Roy and the Russian geologist Vernadsky, who was in Paris at the time.[113]

One of the earliest discussions of the "nous" or "noos" may be found in the writings of the pre-Socratic Greek philosopher who introduced philosophy to Athens, Anaxagoras (500–428 BCE).[114] In developing his philosophy of the infinite interconnectedness of an infinite multitude of imperishable small parts, Anaxagoras concluded the following:

> A single overarching principle is needed to provide unity to the whole system. This principle is *nous*.... *"Nous"* is more related to the concept of mind in the sense of the human mind or reason (though distinct from "logos," which is also sometimes translated as reason). It represents, furthermore, a kind of unity of thought a "thinking thing" in some sense.[115]

The Neoplatonists developed the concept of the *nous* even further 800 years later, which can be found particularly in Plotinus.[116] According to Plotinus, writing in the third century CE, the original Being, the One, emanates the *nous*, the archetype of all manifestations in the visible world of time and space.[117]

> Plotinus presents a philosophy of Unity: unity as unfathomable and transcendent, and unity as omnipresent and immanent.[118]

This Neoplatonist *nous* is accessible to the human mind under certain conditions, and it is what the Neoplatonists termed the *anima mundi* or "world soul" that bridges the *nous* with the material world of time and space.[119] Teilhard's noosphere, as expressed in his numerous essays, corresponds more with the Neoplatonist *anima mundi*.

Teilhard's concept of the noosphere is indeed part of the phenomenal world even as it maintains links to the transcendent, but it is specifically associated with the planets in general and the Earth in particular, with human consciousness evolving within a planetary sphere. Teilhard goes so far as to discuss the possibility of multiple, numerous noospheres, associated with distant planets, and speculates that there may indeed be communication between these multiple noospheres.[120]

Though there had been some controversy over the origin of the word "noosphere," Teilhard confirmed shortly before his death that the word was his own in a letter referring to the recent demise of his friend Édouard Le Roy. In the letter, Teilhard writes:

> "I believe, so far as one can ever tell, that the word 'noosphere' was my invention; but it was he [Le Roy] who launched it."[121]

In a 1951 essay, almost thirty years after first using the term, Teilhard elaborates his mature understanding of the noosphere:

> It is an amazing thing—in less than a million years the human "species" has succeeded in covering the earth: and not only spatially—on this surface that is now completely encircled mankind has completed the construction of a close network of planetary links, so successfully that a special envelope now stretches over the old biosphere. Every day this new

integument grows in strength; it can be clearly recognized and distinguished in every quarter; it is provided with its own system of internal connections and communications—and for this I have for a long time proposed the name of *noosphere*.[122]

In a collection of essays, *The Biosphere and Noosphere Reader*, the editors begin their preface by characterizing the search for the noosphere:

> The noosphere lies at an intersection where science and philosophy meet . . . an interdisciplinary domain of wide interest and high relevance that remains outside the purview of most specialists, but is of major significance for the future of humankind.[123]

The editors present four approaches to Teilhard's concept of the noosphere:

1. The *noosphere* is a product of the biosphere as transformed by human knowledge and action.

2. The *noosphere* represents an ultimate and inevitable sphere of evolution.

3. The *noosphere* is a manifestation of global mind.

4. The *noosphere* is the mental sphere in which change and creativity are inherent although essentially unpredictable.[124]

Locating the Noosphere

At this point we speculate as to where in the physical space–time universe the noosphere might be found. To find the noosphere, let us try a thought experiment and build a likely image of it. Picture in your mind the geometry of the planet Earth. Imagine the heat, approximately 7200° C in the central core.[125] Place your consciousness at the absolute geometric-gravitational central point of the planetary core. Now, begin to slowly move (or rise) outward along a radial line toward the cold of space, noting the temperature drop as you move away from the center of the planet—and stop at the moment you arrive at the temperature 98.2° F, the average human core temperature.

By repeating the above procedure multiple times, with many different radii moving at various angular separations away from the core, a three-dimensional surface mapping, like a mathematical brane or Teilhard's isosphere, will begin to emerge—an infrared energy isosphere to which each human being is linked through an identical resonance frequency.[126]

The shape of this isosphere will likely be highly organic and fractal in appearance, sometimes hovering above the ground on thermoclimes where the "ambient temperature" reaches 98.2° F, while in arctic regions and the oceans it will be located hundreds of feet below the surface of ice or water.

But the noosphere is more than simply a dynamic location on the surface of an isosphere at (or above or below) the rocky surface of the earth. It is energy at the same frequency band as the human body, which has been said to generate approximately 1.3 watts of radiant power with each heartbeat.[127] While we normally think of each heartbeat as simply a pushing of blood through the arteries, it is also radiantly generating infrared electromagnetic energy (the infrared being a range of the spectrum that we often hear dismissively described as "heat").

How might this information be used to substantiate Teilhard's vision of the reality of the noosphere, which would manifest in some planetary energy of consciousness? A chart of global population growth (Fig. 3) indicates that there are currently approximately 7 billion human beings living on the planet.

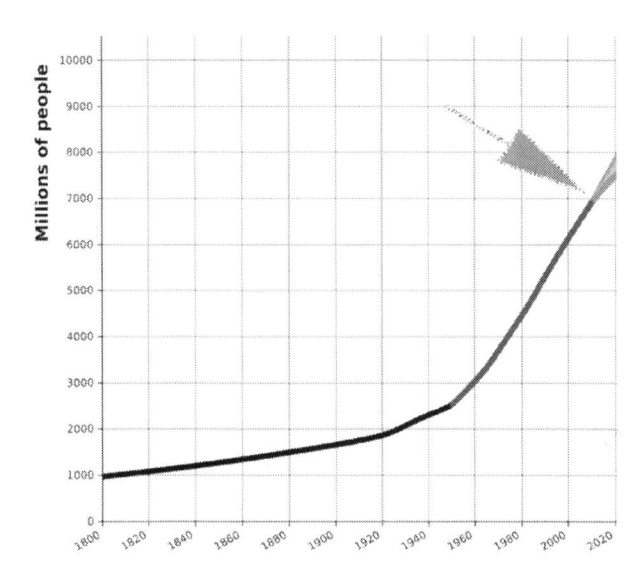

Figure 3. Human population of the Earth since 1800. Graphic by Aetheling (2012). Reprinted under the terms of a Creative Commons Attribution ShareAlike 3.0 Unported license. Image retrieved from Wikimedia Commons.

Accordingly, we can multiply 7 billion humans by the average of 1.3 watts of radiation per human to find the current amount of energy being broadcast by all human hearts: this calculation gives us more than nine gigawatts (9,100,000,000 watts). In Table 1, this amount well surpasses the output of the most powerful radio transmitter in the world ~~at 1,000,000 watts (one megawatt),~~ and even the maximum energy output of the Three Mile Island nuclear power plant's occasional maximum output.

Table 1
Radiant Energy Outputs, Compared

Source of energy	Power
Most powerful radio frequency transmitter on planet[128]	1,000,000 watts
Maximum output of Three Mile Island nuclear reactor[129]	873,000,000 watts

Combined electromagnetic output of human heartbeats	9,100,000,000 watts

It is possible that the nine gigawatts of electromagnetic energy being continuously broadcast by our collective heartbeats may be taking part in a vast energetic interactive resonance with Gaia. Our own collective energy, which transmits in the far infrared in the 10-micron wavelength range (predicted by Wien's Law for our body temperature range) is the part of the geomagnetosphere that is us, the noosphere (the "us" sphere).

Evidence of direct interaction of the electromagnetic energy of the geomagnetosphere with human consciousness can be viewed in Fig. 4.

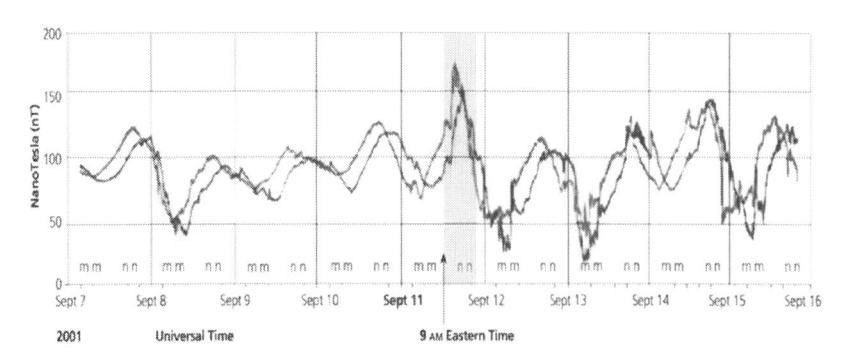

Figure 4. Evidence of a coherent planetary standing wave.[130] Image from McCraty, Deyhle, and Childre, "The Global Coherence Initiative," 75, fig. 10. Reprinted with permission from HeartMath Institute.

Figure 4 shows a chart recording daily data from Geostationary Operational Environmental Satellites and weather satellites in geosynchronous orbit over the United States in the days before, during, and after the September 11, 2001 terrorist attacks. Continuous readings show a marked peak on September 11, 2001, followed by several days of marked disruption in the observed diurnal rhythm of the geomagnetosphere.[131]

In the conclusion of the paper, the authors state, "The study . . . supports the hypothesis that humanity is connected via a global field."[132] Perhaps the same hypothetical "global field" of radiation can be seen in the one Teilhard describes in a 1953 essay, "A Sequel to the Problem of Human Origins":

> Our minds cannot resist the inevitable conclusion that were we, by chance, to possess plates that were sensitive to the specific radiation of the "noospheres" scattered throughout space, it would be *practically certain* that what we saw registered on them would be a cloud of thinking stars.[133]

In early summer of 1923, during Teilhard's expedition into the Ordos desert of Outer Mongolia,[134] he had another major vision, a peak experience later recounted in "The Mass on the World," and of which he commented:

> I see the same thing as I saw long ago at the "front" (which from the human point of view, was the most alive region that existed): one single operation is in process of happening in the world, and it alone can justify our action.[135]

After 18 months in China, Teilhard returned to Paris only to discover that his earlier essay on "original sin" had been discovered by a Jesuit colleague in one of his desk drawers at the Institut Catholique and subsequently forwarded to the Vatican, "where the Holy Office and the Jesuit headquarters already held a file on Teilhard."[136] Reproaching him for having dared to discuss new ways of understanding original sin, the Church authorities (1) insisted that he "sign a pledge to keep silent in the future," (2) permanently revoked his license to teach at the Institut Catholique, where he had been an assistant professor in geology, and (3) asked him to leave Paris.[137] Thus, Teilhard's return to China in 1926 seems to have been at a low point in his career:

> His departure had something of the aspect of a disgrace. He had been removed from Paris by the prudence of his superiors, to whom he had been denounced for propagating dubious ideas, and who feared a censure that would be equally prejudicial to the career of the young scientist and the good name of the Order. Thus he was leaving France under a cloud for an indefinite time, and he saw the momentum of his influence broken just as it was beginning to prove fruitful.[138]

Problems with a previous essay only aggravated the situation. When he sent one of his earliest essays—"Cosmic Life," a 56-page essay written at Dunkirk during Easter week, 1916—to the editors of a Jesuit periodical in Paris, *Etudes,* it was rejected for including such sentences as "The life of Christ mingles with the life-blood of evolution."[139] In the rejection letter, one of the editors explained:

> Your thesis is *exciting* [he used the English word, in the midst of French] and interesting to a high degree.... It is a rich canvas, full of beautiful images. But it is not at all suited for our peaceful readers.[140]

The essay had then been brought to the attention of officials at the Vatican by Teilhard's Jesuit supervisor, Father Claude Chanteur, who expressed strong reservations about giving Teilhard formal admission into the Jesuit Order— but who eventually, perhaps reluctantly, allowed the 37-year-old Teilhard to take his solemn vows on May 26, 1918.[141]

Upon his return to China in 1926, Teilhard made the best of his virtual exile, involving himself deeply in running the Jesuit museum there and accompanying Father Licent on extensive paleontological expeditions into the vast interior of Eastern Mongolia.[142] During the next 20 years, Teilhard travelled extensively between China and Paris, but during the years from 1940 to 1946 he found himself in Peking under Japanese occupation and unable to travel. Instead, he devoted himself to perhaps his most challenging essays on the dynamics of consciousness, including "Centrology," discussed in the following section.

In May 1946, at the end of World War II, Teilhard returned to Paris, where he tried unsuccessfully to obtain permission to publish a major work he had completed in China over a period of several years, *The Human Phenomenon*. While awaiting a reply, Teilhard began giving lectures on his latest philosophical ideas after a hiatus of 22 years, and he soon began to attract the interest of young Jesuit students as well as that of a public that had become more secular and less conservative as a result of the war. While Teilhard scrupulously avoided large venues (he had been forbidden in 1923 to give large public addresses), he fell into hectic activity, alternating between intimate private conversations and semipublic discussions. During one such series of monthly discussions with several Jesuit intellectuals, Teilhard set forth two fundamental points in his philosophy, as recorded by one of the attending priests, Fr. Lejay:[143]

- God acts globally on the whole of evolution and consequently utilizes, in selective fashion, all the possibilities offered by secondary causes.

- Evil is a by-product of evolution, for there is no evolution without groping, without the intervention of chance; consequently, checks and mistakes are always possible.[144]

After the war in Europe, the topic of evil was of great interest not only among intellectuals, but also among the general public.[145] Teilhard's characterization of evil as a part of the process of an evolutionary energy did not sit well with conservative Church authorities, nor did his growing popularity among intellectual Jesuits and the public. He was offered a chair at the College de France, but received word from the Vatican in 1950 that he was not permitted to accept the position. That same year, even his close friends and sympathetic colleagues were censured: "Jesuit academics who had espoused Teilhard's ideas, among them his friend Henri de Lubac, were ordered by the Vatican to leave their positions."[146] Teilhard decided that he could no longer reside in Paris, and after securing a position in New York, he left for travel and, in virtual exile, spent the rest of his life in North America.

In 1954 Teilhard mentioned in a letter to a nephew that when he died, he wished that it might be on Easter Sunday, the quintessential Catholic day for celebrating resurrection and transformation into eternal life.[147] Perhaps this wish can be seen as an example of real psychic precognition, for on April 10, 1955, Teilhard attended Easter services at St. Patrick's Cathedral and enjoyed the Sunday afternoon in company of his close friend Rhoda de Terra and her daughter.[148] Pierre Teilhard de Chardin died while drinking a cup of tea in the front room: "Suddenly, while standing at her window, he fell full length to the floor like a stricken tree."[149] Only a few friends attended his funeral, and only two people accompanied his body on the journey to the cemetery at the Jesuit novitiate of St. Andrews-on-the-Hudson, 60 miles north of New York City.[150]

> Only Pére Leroy and another priest accompanied Teilhard on his last journey. The coffin had to be laid in a temporary vault because the earth was still too frozen for a grave.[151]

Teilhard is buried near the east bank of the Hudson River, under a simple stone inscribed only with his name, dates, and "R. I. P." The small grave remains, but the seminary was sold in 1970; it is now the headquarters of the Culinary Institute of America.[152]

Teilhard's Hyperphysics

Teilhard sees the current human phenomenon of consciousness to be in the early stages of what he terms a "noogenesis," a change of state in human consciousness into a more powerful union, a "joining with other centres of cosmic life to resume the work of universal synthesis on a higher scale."[153] The dynamics of this change and the architecture of consciousness itself is the subject of Teilhard's hyperphysics. Teilhard's ideas are clear, his writing style is straightforward, and his logic transparent; however, appreciation of his more detailed observations on the dynamics of an energy of consciousness requires careful examination of his more technical writing. Teilhard was fascinated by the phenomenon of "change of state," such as when water changes state to become ice, and, in particular, of evolutionary changes of state, such as when matter changes state to become life. But his greatest interest can be seen in potential imminent changes of state in consciousness itself, both human and cosmic, as he observed here in 1937 (note in the quote that Teilhard often uses the words "spirit" and "consciousness" interchangeably):

> The phenomenon of spirit [consciousness] is not therefore a sort of brief flash in the night; it reveals a gradual and systematic passage from the unconscious to the conscious, and from the conscious to the self-conscious. It is a *cosmic change of state*.[154]

Teilhard describes three critical points in the evolutionary arc of consciousness on earth as three changes of state:

- "First the appearance of life whence emerged the biosphere."

- "Then, the emergence of thought which produced the noosphere."

- "Finally, a further metamorphosis: the coming to consciousness of an Omega in the heart of the noosphere."[155]

In his numerous essays Teilhard constructs the picture of a panoramic evolutionary arc: The Earth, having experienced a change of state at the moment when life appeared, experienced another change of state as life erupted into self-reflection (thought) in the biological zenith of *homo sapiens*. Teilhard predicts that this evolutionary arc is now moving toward yet another change of state, and is in the process of transforming human consciousness, collectively, into an even greater "complexity-consciousness,"[156] an "internal centro-complexification,"[157] both in the individual as well as the species, through the process of "centration"[158] or "centrogenesis."[159] These terms have all been constructed and developed by Teilhard to articulate and support his theory, and can be regarded as specific to his theory of hyperphysics. We will examine and clarify these terms by focusing on three essays in which his physics of consciousness, hyperphysics, is set forth:

- "The Phenomenon of Spirit" (1937), written during an ocean voyage

- "Human Energy" (1937), written in Peking

- "Centrology" (1944), written in Peking

While major components of Teilhard's hyperphysics are presented in these three essays, additional insights into the same concepts can be found throughout his many other writings, both published and unpublished.

"The Phenomenon of Spirituality" (1937)

In 1937 Teilhard made the long Pacific voyage from Shanghai to the United States, where he had been invited to receive the Mendel Medal in recognition of his work in paleontology, specifically as one of the discoverers of Peking Man.[160] During this voyage he completed an essay, "The Phenomenon of Spirituality," in which he not only discusses evolution, consciousness, and morality, but begins to articulate details of a hyperphysics of consciousness. In this essay he joins with panpsychist philosopher–scientists from Plato to William James in affirming that it is impossible to deny that consciousness is a part of the natural universe.[161] He also introduces his concept of *centrology*, a basic building block of hyperphysics; a seed from which, nine years later, emerged the cornerstone of Teilhard's hyperphysics, the essay "Centrology: An Essay in a Dialectic of Union," written in Peking in 1944.[162] The richness and diversity of ideas developed in "The Phenomenon of Spirituality" are stunning and wide-ranging. The topics move from evolutionary cosmology to consciousness, morality, and future research, and at the conclusion of the essay, he speaks of the possibility of seeking scientific proof of consciousness as a *centre* of energy:

> Regarding the possibility of proof obtained by direct observation...there must be a means...of recognizing...some psychic effect (radiation or

attraction) specifically connected with the operation of this centre.[163]

In approaching Teilhard's essay, it is important at the outset to consider his frequent use of the terms "spirituality" and "spirit," as opposed to "consciousness." As a Jesuit Catholic priest, Teilhard's free use of the words "spirit" and "spirituality" may be easily understood, though the words are colored with religious overtones. Teilhard often seems to interchange the words "spirit" and "consciousness" in his essays, and often one assumes the terms may be synonymous, but the following passage in another essay, also written in 1937, offers a distinction between "spirit" and "consciousness":

> Human energy presents itself to our view as the term of a vast process in which the whole mass of the universe is involved. In us the evolution of the world towards the spirit becomes conscious.[164]

The first sentence tells us that Teilhard views the universe as a "process" and as a "whole."[165] In the second sentence, Teilhard sees our human state as one in which the "evolution of the world" is becoming "conscious," and in which our human consciousness itself is evolving "towards the spirit." The relationship of spirit to consciousness for Teilhard is reminiscent of the metaphor of the ouroboros snake chasing its tail (see Fig. 5).

Figure 5. The Ouroboros. Graphic by Pelekanos (1478). An image from a late medieval Byzantine Greek alchemical manuscript Reprinted under the terms of a Creative Commons Attribution ShareAlike 3.0 Unported license. Image retrieved from Wikimedia Commons.

However, Teilhard often uses the word "spirit" when "consciousness" would appear to be more appropriate, and henceforth in quoting passages from Teilhard we will provide an alternate reading of "consciousness" via angle brackets where deemed appropriate, as in "the phenomenon of spirit [consciousness] . . . is the thing we know best in the world since we are itself."[166]

In the opening of "The Phenomenon of Spirituality," Teilhard argues that consciousness, whether a force or an energy, should be regarded as a natural, real phenomenon in the universe, worthy of study alongside other equally "real" phenomena that are taken as objects of interest in science (e.g., light, heat, electromagnetism, gravity, etc.):

> Around us, bodies present various qualities: they are warm, colored, electrified, heavy. But also in certain

cases they are living, conscious. Beside the phenomena of heat, light and the rest studied by physics, there is, just as real and *natural*, the *phenomenon of spirituality*.[167]

Teilhard finds it surprising that humans have never truly come to understand this spirit/consciousness in which we are all glaringly immersed:

> The phenomenon of spirit [consciousness] has rightly attracted human attention more than any other. We are coincidental with it. We feel it from within. It is the very thread of which the other phenomena are woven for us. *It is the thing we know best in the world since we are itself*, and it is for us everything. And yet we never come to an understanding concerning the nature of this fundamental element.[168]

Teilhard describes the two most conventional approaches traditionally taken in regarding the phenomenon of consciousness:

1. Religious traditions regard consciousness [spirit], in general, to be of a transcendent nature, not of this physical, space–time world, while by contrast, and

2. Modern science regards consciousness as an epiphenomenon, a unique accident in the recent evolutionary history of the planet.

Teilhard tells us that in this essay he will develop an alternative to these two approaches:

> I propose in these pages to develop a third viewpoint towards which a new physical science and a new philosophy seem to be converging in the present day: that is to say that spirit [consciousness] is neither

super-imposed nor accessory to the cosmos, but that it quite simply represents the higher state assumed in and around us by the primal and indefinable thing that we call, for want of another name, the "stuff of the universe."[169]

Teilhard tells us that the phenomenon of consciousness has been overlooked as an object of study within physical science because, at first sight, the "consciousness portion of the world presents itself in the form of discontinuous, tiny and ephemeral fragments: a bright dust of individualities," while in truth the dimensions of this consciousness ought to be taken as "the dimensions of the universe itself."[170]

But in order to see this, says Teilhard, we need to develop a new form of perception, a new sense with which we may "educate our eyes to perceiving collective realities." Teilhard predicts the development not only of a new form of "direct vision," but the emergence of a previously unsuspected psychic ability, a new sensory mode:

> Men have for long been seeking a means of immediately influencing the bodies and souls around them by their will, and of penetrating them by *a direct vision*. . . . Nothing seems to me more vital, from the point of view of human energy, than the spontaneous appearance and, eventually, the systematic cultivation of such a "cosmic sense."[171]

Teilhard apparently sensed evolutionary transformations through both his direct inner vision and his outer vision; he has critically observed an internal as well as an external nature. Evolution, claims Teilhard, is often accompanied by sudden changes of state, as in water that is seen to become ice or a solution in crystallization—a change of state in "not only molecular or atomic complexity, but interiorization."[172] Teilhard perceives, internally and externally, that in

49

consciousness change of state follows a process of centration or compression. This can be compared with and contrasted to entropy—the movement of expansion, diffusion, and dissipation—and together they can be seen as "two fundamental cosmic movements...which we can grasp experientially."[173] He describes these two contrary movements as the concurrent movement of energy in two directions, the "vitalization" and the "dissipation" of energy, and says that they "are merely the opposite poles of a single cosmic event."[174] Fig. 6 contrasts the two movements of entropy and centration.

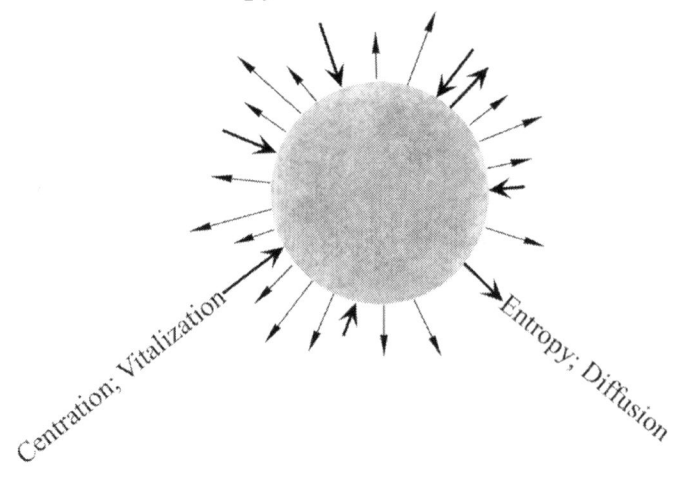

Figure 6. Entropy and centration.

In words that parallel David Bohm's description of an ongoing process of enfolding and unfolding between an implicate and an explicate order, Teilhard describes "the inward furling from which consciousness is born...around a centre...the All becoming self-reflective upon a single consciousness."[175]

At this point he brings up a theme that will arise repeatedly in his later essays, the transcendence of death by the individual personality.[176] Teilhard says that "to become superconscious the fragmented building blocks of man must unite itself with others,"[177] but without losing personalities previously acquired, without losing information. Recall that Teilhard had sensed this phenomenon as a totalization of multiple centres[178] of consciousness, in 1916 at the front.

He goes on to state that humans in general seem to have lost the "faculty of totalization," with the exception of a few mystics who have been able to experience union by dissolution, much like salt in the ocean. But it is union by differentiation that interests Teilhard, not union by dissolution.

> We can see a justification ahead for our hope of a personal immortality . . . without becoming confused with one another . . . to complete ourselves we must pass into a greater than ourselves. . . . In this convergent universe, all the lower centres unite, but by inclusion in a more powerful centre. Therefore they are all preserved and completed by joining together.[179]

Teilhard then turns to the implications of such a theory for morality in a section he calls "Moral Applications." He describes two categories of morality: the "Morality of Balance" and the "Morality of Movement."[180]

Morality of Balance vs. Morality of Movement

The old morality is the morality of balance—an attempt at homeostasis, a "morality that arose largely as an empirical defense of the individual and society."[181] Teilhard goes on to say, "Morality has till now been principally understood as a fixed system of rights and duties intended to establish a static equilibrium."[182] However, in light of the modern discovery of the evolutionary nature of everything in the universe, the human being must be seen as "an element destined to complete himself cosmically in a higher consciousness in process of formation," and thus there is a need for a new morality, a morality of growth (movement) that will foster and catalyze evolutionary change, a growth into a new formation of being.

Teilhard says that new times and a new understanding of the trajectory of life and consciousness implies that while the "moralist was up to now a jurist, or a tight-rope walker," the moralist of the future must "become the technician and engineer of the spiritual [consciousness] energies of the world."[183] He says that for those who see the development of consciousness "as *the* essential phenomenon of nature . . . morality is consequently nothing less than the higher development of mechanics and biology. The world is ultimately constructed by moral forces."[184] Having argued the urgent requirement for a new morality, a morality of growth, Teilhard sets forth "three rules that clearly modify or complete the idea we have of goodness and perfection":

- Good "is what makes for the growth of spirit [consciousness]."

- Good is everything that brings "growth of consciousness to the world."

- "Finally, best is what assures their highest development to the spiritual powers [consciousness] of the earth."[185]

Teilhard summarizes, "Many things seemed to be forbidden by the morality of balance which become virtually permitted or even obligatory by the morality of movement." For example, in following a morality of balance, as long as we follow society's rules, we are permitted to waste our lives in any frivolous pursuit (i.e., in sheer entertainment); whereas under a morality of movement, such things as research through experimentation with psychotropic drugs and participatory exploration of multiple religions would likely be permissible. Disregarding likely disapproval by Vatican censors, Teilhard urges a new human morality of growth (see Table 2) that "will forbid a neutral and 'inoffensive' existence, and compel him strenuously to free his *autonomy* and *personality* to the utmost," and he urges us "to try everything and to force everything in the direction of the greatest consciousness."[186]

Table 2
Morality of Balance versus Morality of Growth

Morality of balance	Morality of growth
Homeostasis; closed.	Evolutionary movement; open.
Fixed rules, rights, and duties to sustain the present.	Whatever fosters growth of consciousness for the future.
Love is subordinate to procreation.	Love gives incalculable spiritual power.
The old moralities of balance are static, powerless to govern the earth.	What is needed is a new morality of movement, of growth.

Note. Data adapted from Teilhard, "The Phenomenon of Spirituality," 105–10. Author's table.

One can see in Table 2 why the more conservative Church authorities might have had some problems with these ideas, but Teilhard is an unapologetic explorer (and a mystic) who unequivocally states:

> The boldest mariners of tomorrow will set out to explore and humanize the mysterious ocean of moral energies . . . our goal is to try everything and to force everything in the direction of the greatest consciousness . . . ever since its beginnings life has been a groping, an adventure, a risk, and general and highest law of morality: to limit force is sin.[187]

At the conclusion of his essay, Teilhard urges us "situate the stuff of the universe in consciousness . . . and to see nature as the development of this same consciousness." He regards the idea of a cosmos as "a moving towards personality," and he concludes with another statement that would likely win him no affection among more conservative elements in the Vatican:

> This is the origin of the present crisis in morality . . . a powerlessness of (old) moralities of balance to govern the earth. It is necessary for the religions to change themselves . . . what we are all more or less lacking at this moment is a new definition of holiness.[188]

Holoflux Theory and Teilhard's "Spirit"

At the heart of this essay, Teilhard introduces a major hypothesis in a key paragraph that is essential to understanding his hyperphysics, and which accords well with the quantum physics of David Bohm, in which the cosmos is seen both as simultaneously unfolding and enfolding:

> Everything that happens in the world, we would say, suggests that the unique centre of consciousness around which the universe is furling could only be formed gradually, through a series of diminishing concentric spheres, each of which engenders the next; each sphere being moreover formed of elementary centres charged with a consciousness that increases as their radius diminishes. By means of this mechanism each newly appearing sphere is charged in its turn with the consciousness developed in the preceding spheres, carries it to a degree higher in each of the elementary centres that compose it, and transmits it a little further on toward the centre of total convergence.[189]

This description can be seen as congruent with the theory of holospheres, in which smaller dimensions converge to the limit found at the Planck holosphere—at which point the implicate order begins.

Teilhard concludes this section by telling us that "the final centre of the whole system appears at the end both as the final sphere and as the centre of all the centres spread over this final sphere."[190] This "centre of all centres" can be understood as Bohm's implicate order, transcending space–time. Teilhard also refers to this centre as "a quantum of consciousness," and tells us that (a) each degree of consciousness at a given moment only exists as "an introduction to a higher consciousness" and (b) this general process is irresistible and irreversible.[191]

If we accept this hypothetical model, says Teilhard, then we are led to two conclusions for the present and for the future:

1. The source of all our difficulties in understanding matter is that it is habitually regarded as inanimate.[192]

2. We are moving towards a higher state of general consciousness . . . other spheres must exist in the future and, inevitably, there exists a supreme centre in which all the personal energy represented by human consciousness must be gathered and "super-personalized."[193]

How might we understand Teilhard's use of the term "spirit" in terms of modern consciousness theory? It is evident that Teilhard's "spirit" appears to be equivalent to holoflux energy as it manifests within Bohm's implicate order. In the holoflux theory,[194] spirit has a *nonlocal* locus embedded within a plenum of Planck-length spherical centers at the granular bottom of space–time, everywhere. Conversely, what is termed consciousness is localized in space–time, manifesting as expanding flux in detectable fields of electromagnetic waves, as illustrated in Fig. 7.

SPIRIT))))) **CONSCIOUSNESS**
NON-LOCAL   LOCAL

Figure 7. Nonlocal spirit versus local consciousness.

Yet they are in relationship—they both exist as part of Bohm's "Wholeness"—and there exists a direct connection between spirit and consciousness through the phenomenon of frequency resonance operating through Fourier transform-like mathematical processes.

It is useful to go topologically further into the holoflux analogy. Imagine the communal locus of Teilhard's "spirit" as it is found within, at the very center of every "point" within space–time. The holoflux process *is* the implicate order, is *one with* the implicate order; "spirit," as implicate order holoflux, has the advantage of being self-superpositioned, fully interconnected, transcendent of the limits of time and space, and can be identified in electrical engineering terms as the frequency domain.

Let us now move outward in scale, bridging the transition zone, the isospheric shell which divides the implicate order from the explicate order. Here we see holoflux emerging from the implicate order as it transforms into space–time energy, flaring forth as waves of spherically vibrating electromagnetic energy. These waves of energy emerge everywhere into space–time from a holoplenum of Planck diameter isospheres. Each isosphere can be seen to encapsulate the entire implicate order, within which the infinity of frequencies from all time and all space are eternally enfolding into a hyper-harmonic flux.

In terms of Bohmian holoflux theory, the first approach to consciousness, the religious, is focused almost exclusively upon an implicate domain, energy as a transcendent flux, and a focus that generally ignores or rejects as unreal the space–time explicate domain; conversely, in the second approach to consciousness, the modern scientific, the focus is upon space–time explicate mode phenomena, one that completely ignores the possible reality of a non-space–time domain.

Teilhard proposes an alternative to these two, seemingly mutually exclusive, approaches:

> I propose in these pages to develop a third viewpoint towards which a new physical science and a new philosophy seem to be converging at the present day: that is to say that spirit is neither super-imposed nor accessory to the cosmos, but that it quite simply represents the higher state assumed in and around us by the primal and indefinable thing that we call, for want of a better name, the "stuff of the universe." Nothing more; and also nothing less. Spirit is neither a meta-phenomenon nor an epi-phenomenon; it is *the* phenomenon.[195]

Evidence of Teilhard's "spirit," or "*the* phenomenon," can be seen in the "Holy Spirit" from Teilhard's Catholic teaching of the Holy Trinity. to It is in accord with the sub-quantum holoflux model that views the Whole as one single energy, processing within and between two primary domains: a space–time domain, and a spectral domain.

In Fig. 8 can be seen a complete Planck diagram of the Holy Trinity highlighting Teilhard's distinction between *tangential consciousness* and *axial consciousness* mapped by Bohm's distinction between a nonlocal (implicate) order and a local (explicate) order in space and time.

The Father → **Axial Consciousness** NON-LOCAL — IMPLICATE ORDER (*Spectral*) — **Holoflux Energy** (frequency-phase)

The Holy Spirit — *Fourier Transform*

The Son → **Tangential Consciousness** LOCAL — EXPLICATE ORDER (*Space-time*) — **Electromagnetic Energy** (frequency-phase in space-time)

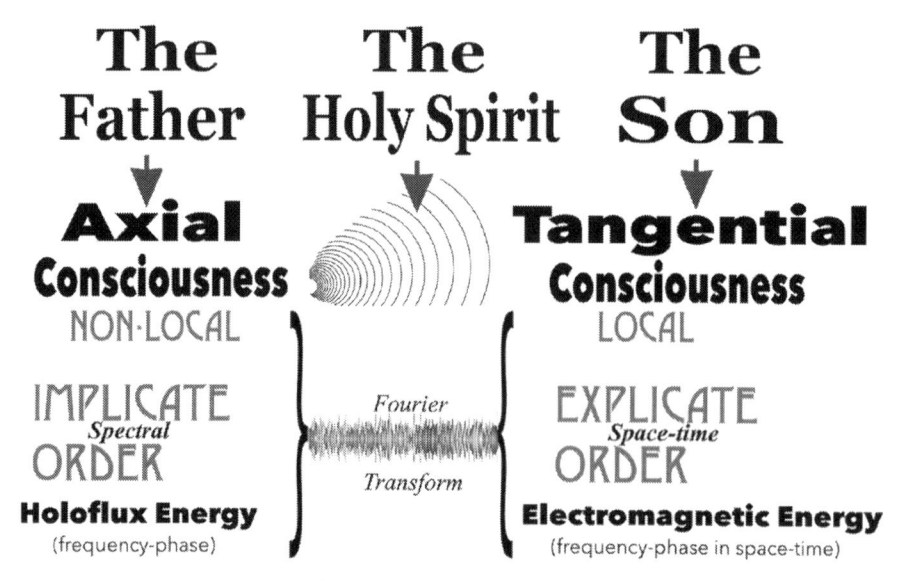

Figure 8. A Planck Diagram of the Holy Trinity.

The identifies "spirit" in the center, bridging the nonlocal implicate order and the local explicate order. Between the two orders that make up the Whole, we see the energy process of the Fourier Transform as the Holy Spirit—possibly the mysterious "dark energy" being sought by physicists.[196] Conversely, "consciousness" can be seen on the right in the space–time region, manifesting as the energy of consciousness in time and in space (i.e., a Cosmic Christ consciousness), and also identified here as electromagnetic energy.

A Christian approach to the diagram would consider God the Father as hypostasis of the Non-Local Implicate Order, the Holy Spirit as hypostasis of continuous two-way Fourier transforms, and the Son as physically manifest consciousness within space and time.

Summary of Teilhard de Chardin's Trinity

The Omega Point → God the Father, the Logos
Centro-Complexity → The Cosmic Christ
Energy → The Holy Spirit

"Human Energy" (1937)

In "Human Energy," an essay written in Peking that same year, Teilhard describes three forms of energy and implies that modern science only considers the first two while ignoring the third. He identifies these three forms as

- Incorporated energy,
- Controlled energy, and
- Spiritualized [conscious] energy.

Incorporated energy manifests in rocks, crystals, neurons, and so on. Controlled energy is that generated by humans and used to thermodynamically and electrically power human devices. Energy of the third kind, Teilhard's "spiritualized energy," or as we might say, the "energy of consciousness," is the primary subject of his essay, hence "Human Energy."[197]

In this essay, Teilhard proposes that each human "represents a cosmic nucleus ... radiating around it waves of organization and excitation within matter."[198] Teilhard immediately suggests, based it seems upon his own experience, that these radiations can be perceived by human beings, and he makes reference to the need for development of a special psychic mode of perception:

> This perception of a natural psychic unity higher than our "souls" requires, *as I know from experience*, a special quality and training in the observer. Like all broad scientific perspectives it is the product of a prolonged reflexion, leading to the discovery of *a deep cosmic sense.*[199]

Teilhard warns that it is a matter of perception, of tuning, of intent. He says that we are like a cell that can see nothing but other cells, but there are more complex configurations of being if we only can learn how to join with them. He says that "the thoughts of individuals . . . form from the linked multiplicity, a single spirit of the earth," and that he sees humanity continuing to evolve "in the direction of a decisive expansion of our ancient powers reinforced by the acquisition of certain new faculties of consciousness."[200] Teilhard emphasizes that this growth is not a walk of random chance; it unfolds within a universe that is alive with an energy synonymous with the mystery we call love or allurement:

> Love by the boundless possibilities of intuition and communication it contains, penetrates the unknown; it will take its place in the mysterious future, with the group of new faculties and consciousnesses that is awaiting us.[201]

Here he expresses a consideration missing in most physical descriptions of energy, the category of "love," something that Teilhard includes as perhaps the most real, fundamental manifestation of energy in his hyperphysical theories. As early as 1931 in "The Spirit of the Earth," Teilhard had referred to an energy of consciousness, of sensation, of love, as manifesting in a spectrum (much as Jung, in 1946, used the imagery of the spectrum to characterize the energy of the psyche).[202] Teilhard says that "Love is a sacred reserve of energy; it is the blood of spiritual evolution."[203]

> Hominized love is distinct from all other love, because the "spectrum" of its warm and penetrating light is marvelously enriched. No longer only a unique and periodic attraction for purposes of material fertility; but an unbounded and continuous possibility of contact between minds rather than bodies; the play of countless subtle antennae seeking one another.[204]

Teilhard sees this organic love-consciousness energy growing more complex and changing through some natural if currently unknown evolutionary process, but he is confident that there will be an eventual mastery and understanding of this same phenomenon (conscious love) in terms of physics.

Accordingly, he stresses the importance of those engaged in scientific research to turn their focus upon the human phenomenon of consciousness.

He is hopeful, telling us with conviction that "physics will surely isolate and master the secret that lies at the heart of metaphysics"; it will accelerate this evolution toward the emergence of a new cosmic sense:

> Nothing seems to me more vital, from the point of view of human energy, than the spontaneous appearance and, eventually, the systematic cultivation of such a "cosmic sense."[205]

One in Many: The Noosphere

In a section entitled "Organization of Total Human Energy: The Common Human Soul," Teilhard discusses his concept of the noosphere, and sees in the process of "raising men to the explicit perception of their 'molecular' nature" that the possibility opens for them to "cease to be closed individuals, to become parts ... to be integrated in the total energy of the noosphere."[206] But Teilhard is at pains to reassure the reader that this does not imply the loss of individuality, and he points out that individual human souls (the quanta of consciousness) are not like gas molecules, "anonymous and interchangeable corpuscles"—the formation of the noosphere requires, on the contrary, a "maximum of personality" to be manifest through each human individual sub contribution:

> The utility of each nucleus of human energy in relation to the whole depends on what is unique . . . in the achievement of each.[207]

Assuming that consciousness is evolving and the material universe is evolving as well, Teilhard wonders where might the energy come from that guides the coalescing centro-complexity into such exquisite configurations, and he wonders what might be the nature of energy within this evolution (i.e., what is "informing" and "powering" this evolutionary process?). His answer can be found in a section he calls "The Maintenance of Human Energy and 'The Cosmic Point Omega.'" He explains that such energy is axial, that it "is found to be fed by a particular current" flowing from the center, the Omega point, which he calls a "tension of consciousness."[208]

Here Teilhard makes a diversion into a subject he repeatedly brings up, the continuation of the centres of personality after physical death. He says,

> Reflective action and the expectation of total disappearance are *cosmically incompatible* . . . death leaves some part of ourselves in some way, to which we can turn with devotion and interest, as to a portion of the absolute . . . as *imperishable*.[209]

He points out that cosmic evolution is a work of "*personal nature*," and that we are each a unique "centre of personal stuff totalizing, in itself, the essence of our personalities . . . the universal centre of attraction"; at this point he begins to discuss the "centre of psychic convergence," the noosphere, and brings up the image of the sphere.[210]

> "The totality of a sphere is just as present in its centre, which takes the form of a point, as spread over its whole surface."[211]

What are the implications in Teilhard's statement, "the totality of a sphere is just as present in its center?" We could say that it implies a sharing of information storage between the isosphere in space–time and the implicate order at the center (Wheeler's qubits of conscious information spread over the surface of a sphere would be seen here be in resonance with the implicate center). Next, Teilhard poses a question whose solution appears to corroborate the concept of an implicate order within the quantum holosphere, and he concludes with his famous dictum, "union differentiates":

> Now why should it be strange for the universe to have a centre, that is to say to collect itself to the same degree in a single consciousness, if its totality is already partially reflected in each of our particular consciousnesses? . . . Union, the true upward union in the spirit [consciousness], ends by establishing the elements it dominates in their own perfection. *Union differentiates.*[212]

Not only are each of the centres of consciousness preserved in their union, they are *evolutionarily enhanced*; the n centres join. But, in that joining, although they retain their own personalities, an additional personality ($n + 1$) is formed, and "*since there is no fusion or dissolution* of the elementary personalities, the centre in which they join *must necessarily be distinct from them, that is to say have its own personality.*"[213]

It is at this point in his essay that Teilhard introduces the term Omega, describing it as the cosmic point of total synthesis without which "the world would not function" and outlining its relationship to the noosphere:

> The noosphere in fact *physically* requires, for its maintenance and functioning . . . the unifying influence of a *distinct* center of super-personality . . . a centre different from all the other

centres which it "super-centres" by assimilation: a personality distinct from all the personalities it perfects by uniting with them.... Consideration of this Omega will allow us to define more completely... the hidden nature of what we have till now called, vaguely enough, "human energy."[214]

The Omega Point

The concept of Omega or the Omega point is central to Teilhard de Chardin's architecture of hyperphysics. According to his close friend Henri de Lubac, Teilhard's first use of the term can be found in one of his earliest essays:

> In the first essay that was entitled *Mon Univers* (1916) he carefully distinguishes, in order to study their relationships, "Omicron, the natural term of human and cosmic progress," from "Omega, the supernatural term of the Kingdom of God" or "Plenitude of Christ." Later, he was to abandon this particular terminology, but he retained the distinction it expressed.[215]

Twenty years later Teilhard was using the term in a more secular, scientific context, as seen here at the close of a lecture delivered at the French Embassy in Peking on March 10, 1945.[216]

> Ahead of, or rather in the heart of, a universe prolonged along its axis of complexity, there exists a ... centre of convergence ... let us call it the *point Omega*.[217]

Teilhard devotes an entire section to "The Attributes of the Omega Point" in his book, *The Human Phenomenon*, begun in Paris in 1939 and completed in China during World War II.

In a section originally appearing in his first draft as "Spirit and Entropy," Teilhard says of Omega:

> Expressed in terms of internal energy, the cosmic function of Omega consists in initiating and maintaining the unanimity of the world's reflective particles under its radiation. But how could it carry out this action if it were not somehow already... *right here and now*?... Autonomy, actuality, irreversibility and finally, transcendence are the four attributes of Omega... Omega is the principle we needed to explain both the steady advance of things toward more consciousness and the paradoxical solidity of what is most fragile.... Something in the cosmos, therefore, escapes entropy—and does so more and more.[218]

An important element of Teilhard's model of human energy lies in his understanding that consciousness can be expressed in thermodynamic terms. In the essay "Human Energy," in a section titled "V. THE MAINTENANCE OF HUMAN ENERGY AND 'THE COSMIC POINT OMEGA,'" Teilhard describes how an axial form of this heat energy powers the current of conscious human energy. Teilhard describes the generation of this current:

> Considered in its organic material zones, human energy obeys the laws of physics and draws quite naturally on the reserves of heat available in nature. But studied in its axial, spiritualized form, it is found to be fed by a particular current (of which thermodynamics might well be, after all, no more than a statistical echo), which, for want of a better name, we will call "tension of consciousness."[219]

Teilhard here once again links thermodynamics to the phenomenon of consciousness, and he goes on to refute the

65

widespread scientific paradigm of consciousness as a mere epiphenomenon of the material universe:

> We still persist in regarding the physical as constituting the "true" phenomenon in the universe, and the psychic as a sort of epiphenomenon ... we should consider the whole of thermodynamics as an unstable and ephemeral by-effect of the concentration on itself of what we call "consciousness."[220]

Supported by the thesis of this dissertation, it is reasonable to consider Teilhard's Omega Point, when resolved down to the smallest possible dimension known to physics, as equivalent to a "Planck holosphere," which is discussed in Chapter 5.

In one of his last essays, "The Nature of the Point Omega," Teilhard states that it is in the noosphere that all is truly preserved, for it is here that all experience is eternally gathered and saved:

> In convergent cosmogenesis, as I have said, everything happens as if the preservable contents of the world were gathered and consolidated, by evolution, at the centre of the sphere representing the universe ... a cosmic convergence ... to bind objectively to the real and already existing centre.[221]

Here we can see, again, a congruence between Teilhard's process viewed as a convergent cosmogenesis and Bohm's process, seen as an enfolding of the explicate into an implicate domain.

Teilhard concludes the essay "Human Energy" with a highly optimistic observation, revealing once again his lifelong fascination with the concept of the human personality's mode of survival beyond biological death:

The principle of the conservation of personality signifies that each individual nucleus of personality, once formed, is forever constituted as "itself"; so that, in the supreme personality that is the crown of the universe, all elementary personalities that have appeared in the course of evolution must be present again in a distinct (though super-personalized) state ... each elementary person contains something *unique and untransmittable* in his essence.[222]

"Centrology: Dialectics of Union" (1944)

During the Japanese occupation of China, Teilhard's anthropological work was severely curtailed, and he found himself with time to develop his more abstract ideas, which he expressed systematically and in great detail in his 1944 essay, "Centrology," written under somewhat stark wartime conditions during his Peking confinement. At the beginning of his essay, he boldly states what he considers to be the scientific nature of this essay: "It is not an abstract metaphysics, but a realist ultraphysics of union."[223]

Teilhard opens his essay with an immediate discussion of "Centres and Centro-Complexity," describing how in living elements of the biosphere we find a continuation of the "granular (atomic molecular)" structure of the universe, and that, in fact, the human body "is simply a 'super-molecule.'"[224] However, unlike conventional physicists, who see cosmic particles as sources or centers of radiation and then map that radiation in the space–time domain, Teilhard places the focus of his inquiry on the "within" of each so-called particle. According to Teilhard, the space–time particles are not only centers of origination of radiation; each one of them also "has" a within and "is" a within—a within that is a mode of consciousness, a psychic centre:

> They are psychic centres, infinitesimal psychic centres of the universe... in other words, consciousness is a universal molecular property.[225]

Teilhard goes further to claim that an increase in consciousness can be found associated with an increase in "centro-complexity," and he defines "the coefficient of centro-complexity" as "the true absolute measure of being in the beings that surround us."[226] Teilhard describes biology as "simply the physics of very large complexes."[227]

He points out that the atomic complexity of a virus is of the order of 10^5 atomic particles, and this complexity increases dramatically by the time we reach the size of a cell at 10^{10}—but in the brains of large mammals, complexity has multiplied to 10^{20} particles.[228]

Teilhard states that "if the universe is observed in its true and essential movement through time, it represents a system which is in a process of internal centro-complexification," and asserts a definition of evolution to be "a transition from a lower to a higher state of centro-complexity."[229]

In his essay, "Man's Place in the Universe," Teilhard had argued that existence entails three infinities: the infinite large, the infinite small, and the infinite complex, and he illustrates this with the chart reproduced in Fig. 9.[230] Using data from objects in nature, Teilhard plots a curve with two axes: a vertical y-axis scaled in Size (length in centimeters), and a horizontal x-axis on which is measured increases in Complexity (total number of atoms per object). Note that both scales are calibrated in base 10 logarithms. The curve plots size versus complexity for various natural entities, named on both axes.

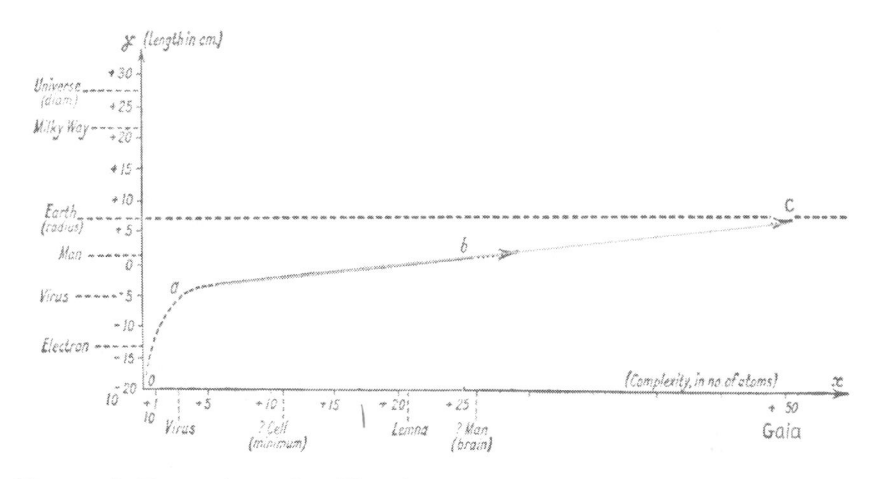

Figure 9. Extension of Teilhard's natural curve of complexities.[231]

Points "a" and "b" on the plot indicate where Teilhard believes "state changes of consciousness" have occurred. Point "a" marks the emergence of life, and point "b" indicates the emergence of reflective consciousness (i.e., thought, being able to think about thinking).

While Teilhard does not discuss the arrow extending the curve to the right, the implication is clear if we mentally plot the value for the Complexity of Earth, which has been estimated to consist of 1.33×10^{50} atoms.[232] Accordingly, we have increased the width of Teilhard's horizontal axis scale, which in his own notebook stops at the human brain's +25 atoms, and have doubled the *x* range to the Earth's +50 atoms. At +50 the curve in Fig. 30 has been extrapolated to intersect Teilhard's converging curve at point "c," marking a planetary change of state, a state described here by Teilhard as an awakening of a consciousness common to the whole earth:

> We can see it only as a *state of unanimity*: such a state, however, that in it each grain of thought, now taken to the extreme limit of its individual consciousness, will simply be the incommunicable, partial, elementary expression of a total

69

consciousness which is common to the whole earth, and specific to the earth: *a spirit* [consciousness] *of the earth.*[233]

Elsewhere, Teilhard has described the importance of the concept of reflection (alternately translated into English as reflexion) and this is associated with point "b" on the complexity chart; the concept also applies to a projected point "c", which would be a change of state for the consciousness of the planet, a noospheric "reflection":

> "Reflection," as the word itself indicates, is the power acquired by a consciousness of turning in on itself and taking possession of itself *as an object* endowed with its own particular consistency and value: no longer only to know something but to know *itself*; no longer only to know, but to know that it knows.[234]

Teilhard's chart thus supports the first general conclusion in his essay on "Centrology," that the universe is in a state of internal "centro-complexification," and that in this "transition from a lower to a higher state of centro-complexity," we see a concomitant increase in complexity-consciousness in a process that Teilhard terms cosmogenesis through centrogenesis.[235]

From his earliest essays, Teilhard sees the planet itself as an evolving, larger entity, out of which humanity has sprung and to which humanity is adding new capabilities. Teilhard presents geological and zoological evidence of the planet Earth as an evolving lifeform,[236] a global being in the transitional process of awakening into a planetary state of reflective self-consciousness. He identifies a distinct axis of successive forms, layers of increasing complexity and centrification running from geogenesis through biogenesis and beyond into psychogenesis; this axis, he insists, can be seen continuing in the present noetic awakening that it is life itself that is engendering the birth of a new mode of planetary consciousness, comprising an entity that he himself has named the noosphere.[237]

He speculates that eventually "life might use its ingenuity to force the gates of its terrestrial prison . . . by establishing a connection psyche to psyche with other focal points of consciousness across space," and notes "the possibility of 'centre-to-centre' contacts between perfect centres."[238]

But it is not only the planet itself that is evolving for Teilhard. He also views consciousness in humanity as evolving and thus sees the human species accelerating toward an evolutionary threshold, where it will experience the nature of energy and self-reflection in ever newer ways while feeling itself drawn magnetically toward new states of greater cohesion and complexity, not only of radiant physical energy, which he terms "the tangential component," but of an increasingly conscious, psychic flow, the spiritual or "radial component" of energy.[239] He even senses an imminent transformation in the biophysical gateway, the human brain, in which he foresees form and function itself complexifying past the point of isolated self-reflection:

> Is there not in fact, beyond the isolated brain, a still higher possible complex: by that I mean a sort of "brain" of associated brains? . . . . From this point of view, the natural evolution of the biosphere is not only continued in what I have called Noosphere, but assumes in it a strictly convergent form which, towards its peak, produces a point of maturation (or of collective reflection).[240]

Another term used by Teilhard in describing this process is "convergence." He states, "in the organo-psychic field of centro-complexity, the world is convergent; the isospheres are simply a system of waves which as time goes on (and it is they which measure time) close up around Omega point"; the world, according to Teilhard, is moving continuously in "a transition from a lower to a higher state of centro-complexity."[241]

Centrogenesis

Teilhard coins a new term, "centrogenesis," to encapsulate this process. In "Centrology," Teilhard begins his discussion of centrogenesis by claiming that the universe is made up of psychic nuclei, similar to the theory of monads developed by Gottfried Wilhelm Leibniz. *Monads* were described by Leibniz as being the most basic, fundamental entities of which the cosmos is constructed (an idea seen here as a precursor to the model of holospheres in the holoplenum); however, in his theory, the monads are completely independent of one another, though in complete harmony.[242] Unlike the monads of Leibniz, Teilhard's nuclei are interconnected in three simultaneous ways.[243] These relationships are as follows:

- Tangentially—"on the surface of an isosphere";

- Radially—"through nuclei of lower centro-complexity" (n^1, n^2, etc.); and

- Radially—"inwardly, creating an isosphere of a higher order" ($n + 1$).

Teilhard describes these elementary cosmic centres as "partially themselves" and "partially the same thing." Fig. 10 presents four drawings by Teilhard that appear at the beginning of his essay on "Centrology."

Figure 1. Diagram symbolizing the principle phases of centrogenesis (convergence of the universe along its axis of centro-complexity or personalization).

Note the concentric system of isospheres (surfaces of equal centro-complexity), subdivided into three zones by the two critical surfaces of centration and reflection (cf. sections 9 and 13).

Omega point is at the centre.

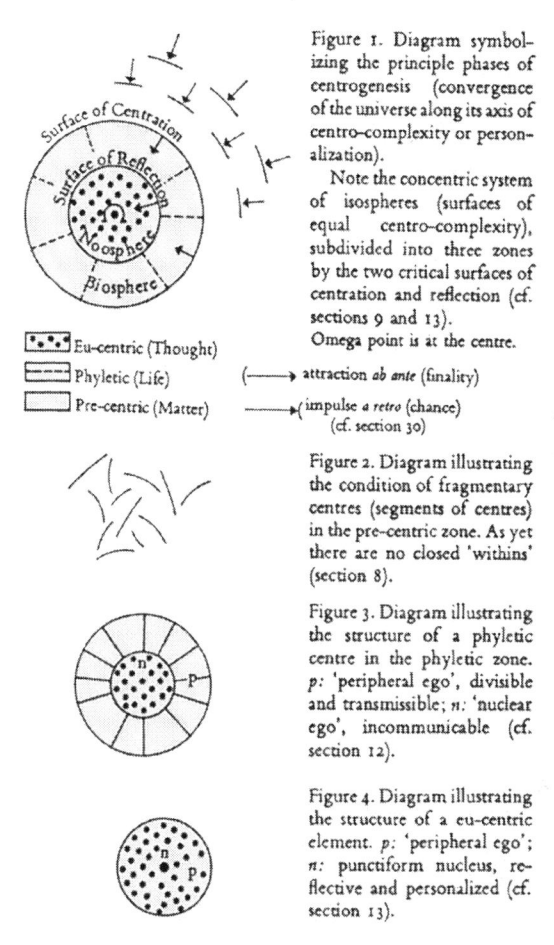

Eu-centric (Thought)
Phyletic (Life)
Pre-centric (Matter)

⟶ attraction *ab ante* (finality)

⟵ impulse *a retro* (chance) (cf. section 30)

Figure 2. Diagram illustrating the condition of fragmentary centres (segments of centres) in the pre-centric zone. As yet there are no closed 'withins' (section 8).

Figure 3. Diagram illustrating the structure of a phyletic centre in the phyletic zone. *p:* 'peripheral ego', divisible and transmissible; *n:* 'nuclear ego', incommunicable (cf. section 12).

Figure 4. Diagram illustrating the structure of a eu-centric element. *p:* 'peripheral ego'; *n:* punctiform nucleus, reflective and personalized (cf. section 13).

Figure 10. Teilhard's Figures 1 through 4 in "Centrology."[244]

Three of Teilhard's images (Figures 2, 3, and 4) depict the three stages of centrogenesis. Here, we can see the condition of "fragmentary centres (segments of centres)" not yet enclosed in isospheric configurations, and still devoid of what Teilhard calls "personality." These are elements that he terms "pre-centric" fragments, having no "withins."[245]

More evolved is the second image from the bottom, which reveals *phyletic centricity*, a change of state brought about by the self-closing of numerous fragmentary centers, which he defines as "life" and which manifests as phylum.[246] In regarding

73

this state, Teilhard brings up two questions. He asks, "How can we conceive the passage and communication of a 'within' from mother-cell to daughter-cell?"—and then asks, "Under what conditions is the phylum provided the greatest possible richness and variety for the evolutionary transmission of successful properties?"[247]

To answer the first question, Teilhard observes that there are "two sorts of ego in each phyletic centre, a nuclear ego ... and a peripheral ego."[248] The *peripheral ego* is incompletely individualized and separate; according to Teilhard, it is therefore divisible and can be shared through replication or association. Teilhard's then explains how the second ego, the *nuclear ego*, communicates:

> It is in virtue of the arrival at zero of its centric diameter that the living centre, in its turn, attains the condition and dignity of a "grain of thought."[249]

Thus, the particular phyletic centre (consisting of a peripheral ego and a nuclear ego) retains access to all of the information ever associated with the particular phylum through resonance among phyletic isospheres (nuclear egos).

This is in agreement with both Sheldrake's theory of morphic resonance and Bohm's quantum cosmology, as it provides a mechanism whereby speciation information may be shared through resonance and transferred into the explicate domain via the implicate domain—and vice versa.[250] Since the implicate order of the nuclear ego is nondual (outside of the space–time domain), it has random access to information generated in *all time* and *all space*, and is thereby able to apply total information in its processing. Reflective consciousness is also a characteristic of this phyletic center, and the typical human personality can be here identified with Teilhard's "peripheral ego," while Omega provides a guiding force via centrogenesis (Bohm's quantum potential function, Q).

To answer his second question (how does the phylum provided the greatest possible richness and variety for evolutionary growth?), Teilhard identifies a "two-fold complexity"—one spatial and the other temporal. Spatial complexity refers to the spread of the phylum over the surface of its isosphere, the creation of a population of phyletic centres that gathers experience and mutates in the ever-changing environment. At the same time, the action of temporal complexity provides the vast number of "trials" over the myriads of generations of which the phylum's ancestors represent the total sum.[251]

At the bottom of Fig. 12 we see Teilhard's final figure, the "structure of a eu-centric element," as a major and perhaps ultimate "change of state" in the emerging process—a reflection of consciousness in the noosphere, a reflective connection with Omega.[252] In the typical human grain of thought, "reflection" has not yet reached a resonance with Omega. However, it is possible to effect in the individual, as Teilhard says, a "eu-centered, 'point-like' focus ... and this is enough to allow the appearance of a series of new phenomena in the later advances of centrogenesis."[253] It is not difficult to assume that the "point-like focus" recommended here by Teilhard is a reference to his own direct experience in effectuating such a focus, his own participatory experience of consciousness.

Teilhard laments that while humans are generally reflective, only a few (as of yet) have been able to integrally connect with the punctiform nucleus, Omega; but those able to connect for any duration find that they now "possess the sense of irreversibility," a conviction that makes "an escape from total death ... possible for a personalized being."[254] At this point, says Teilhard, "Welded together in this way, the noosphere, *taken as a whole*, begins to behave tangentially, like a single megacentre ... ontogenesis of collective consciousness and human memory."[255] Here, Teilhard makes a prediction, stating

75

that the evolution of human society on the planet will eventually lead to the following:

> the accelerated impetus of an earth in which preoccupation with production for the sake of well-being will have given way to the passion for the discovery for the sake of fuller being—the super-personalization of a super-humanity that has become super-conscious of itself in Omega.[256]

In a psychically convergent universe, the process of a reflective connection of the peripheral, phyletic ego with the central, eu-centric ego ultimately leads to a "final concentration upon itself of the noosphere," Omega.

> Omega appears to us fundamentally as the centre which is defined by the final concentration upon itself of the noosphere—and indirectly, of all the isospheres that precede it.[257]

"All the isospheres that precede it" in time and space, of course, are the isospheres that are ourselves, our ancestors, and other centers of phyletic centro-complexity. When a locus of fragmentary centers closes, joining together to form a phyletic center, the newly formed noosphere experiences a state change and awakens. From that point, moving forward in space and time, the phyletic noosphere evolves through a series of internal noospheres, growing higher in energy and complexity, until it reaches its ultimate "final concentration" at Omega, as Teilhard states: "In Omega then, a *maximum complexity*, cosmic in extent, coincides with a *maximum cosmic centricity*."[258] In other words, at the heart of matter, at the Omega point, Teilhard tells us that maximum complexity equals maximum centricity.

Teilhard refers to the centre as "a quantum of consciousness," and tells us that each degree of consciousness at a given moment only exists as "an introduction to a higher consciousness." [259] He says that this general process is irresistible and irreversible.[260]

> The initial quantum of consciousness contained in our terrestrial world is not formed merely of an aggregate of particles caught fortuitously in the same net. It represents a correlated mass of infinitesimal centres structurally bound together by the conditions of their origin and development.[261]

Moving forward in his essay on centrology, Teilhard goes on to describe four attributes of Omega as:

- Personal
- Individual
- Already partially actual (space–time energy)
- Partially transcendent (nondual)[262]

It is personal, "since it is centricity that makes beings personal" and "Omega is supremely centred."[263] It is individual, because it is "distinct from (which does not mean cut off from) *the lower personal centres* which it super-centres."[264] These lower centres are the various phyletic, peripheral egos, each of which is uniquely individual yet able to join with Omega without losing their individuated personality; in fact, it is in the relationship, the resonance with Omega, that the very uniqueness of the individual is highlighted (i.e., "union differentiates").

Omega is both "partially actual" and partially transcendent." The relationship is one that Teilhard characterizes as "a 'bi-polar' union" of the emerged and the emergent. It is partially transcendent beyond the very center of space–time, within the Bohmian implicate order. There, all is "partially transcendent of the evolution that culminates in it," and it is there that all space–time experience is gathered—in the partially transcendent—in continuous communication via a mathematically dynamic process. Otherwise, Teilhard tells us, there would not "be the basis for the hopes of irreversibility."[265]

It is Omega that provides the momentum for centrogenesis:

> Drawn by its magnetism and formed in its image, the elementary cosmic centres are constituted and grow deeper in the matrix of their complexity. Moreover, gathered up by Omega, these same centres enter into immortality from the very moment when they become eu-centric and so structurally capable of entering into contact, centre to centre.[266]

Centrology and Complexity: Being and Union

At this point in his essay, Teilhard inserts what he calls "A Note on the 'Formal Effect' of Complexity," in which he examines the underlying roots of his assertion that consciousness *increases* with complexity in union (centro-complexity), and he states that an understanding of this phenomenon has come to him "experientially."[267] Teilhard sets forth, in two Latin propositions, the fundamental ontological relationship between being and union:

1. One is passive:
    "*Plus esse est a (or ex) pluribus uniri.*"

2. The other is active:
    "*Plus esse est plus plura unire.*"

Plus esse can be translated as "more being," "growth in being," or "being increases," but from the context of this essay the phrase *plus esse* might be translated as "consciousness increases."[268] Thus, Teilhard describes a bi-modal process of an increasing conscious in the universe: active and passive.

In the first proposition, the verb *uniri* is in the passive voice, "be united," and in context can be translated as "become one, become a center." The *a/ex* prepositions, often used interchangeably in Latin, indicate "out of" and "from." Thus, *a pluribus* can be translated "out of many, from many," and accordingly the first proposition may be translated as "A new conscious center grows by many being joined."

In the second proposition, however, the verb *unire* is in the active voice, (i.e., "unite"), which in context can be translated as "make a centered unity" of *plura* (literally, "more/many things"). Thus, the second proposition can be translated as "A new consciousness center grows by many uniting." Teilhard then applies these two propositions to the following stages of centro-complex evolution:

1. The appearance of life through association of fragments of centres.

2. The deepening of phyletic centres.

3. The emergence of reflective centres.

In the first instance, for a state change occurring in the domain of pre-life, Teilhard again formulates a metaphysical axiom in Latin: *Centrum ex elementis centri*, which translates as "The Center out of elements of the center." In this domain, Centres are "built up additively, through the fitting together and gradual fusing of 'segments' of centres."[269] This is a passive growth.

In the second stage, Teilhard says, "being born from an egg (*centrum a centro*) complexifies upon itself by cellular multiplication." Here, each centre complexifies itself by increasing its own depth of complexity.[270] Here, the active growth emerges, a growth in part directed by the centre. A similar pattern can be seen in Bohm's quantum potential function, a guiding energy from within the implicate order within Teilhard's Omega point.

Finally, it is in the eu-centric that this quantum potential metaphysical process becomes super-active and, as Teilhard says, it is from "the noospheric centre, Omega" that there emerges "*Centrum super centra*," translated as "a new Centre emerges from an old centre."[271] Teilhard is saying here that Omega is not simply the sum of components, but something *new*, a unique entity bursting forth:

> In the eu-centric domain, the noospheric centre Omega, is not born from the confluence of human "egos," but emerges from their organic totality, like a spark that leaps the gap between the transcendent side of Omega and the "point" of a perfectly centered universe.[272]

Teilhard describes how, for individual human phyletic "egos," it may be possible to go beyond the present general evolutionary stage of consciousness, developed through the general societal drift of hominization through time. Teilhard explains how such an evolutionary leap might be accomplished:

> This can be envisaged in two ways, either by *connecting up neurones* that are already ready to function but have not yet been brought into service (as though held in reserve), in certain already located areas of the brain, where it is simply a matter of arousing them to activity; or, who can say?, by direct (mechanical, chemical or biological) stimulation of new arrangements.[273]

In his phrase "direct stimulation," we can imagine a range of approaches which might be used to catalyze the evolutionary growth and transformation of consciousness within an individual, who would then experience what Teilhard terms an "Ultra-hominization" of reflective consciousness, evolutionarily beyond that of the currently conventional ranges of human experience.

His first suggestion, "connecting up neurones that are already ready to function," might be seen as a catalysis by birth (genetic predisposition), accidental circumstances (serendipitous encounters with the sublime), or specific psycho-physical techniques (e.g., prayer, yoga, physical exercises, special diets, fasting, sweat lodges, etc.); but Teilhard goes even further to suggest that the evolutionary process might be boosted within the individual human personality "by direct (mechanical, chemical, or biological) stimulation," and here we are reminded of exploration and critical experimentation with psychotropic drugs (psilocybin mushrooms, LSD, cannabis, ayahuasca, etc.) or through direct energy-stimulation devices, as can be seen in the recent technologies of transcranial magnetic stimulation or transcranial direct current stimulation.[274]

Similarly, but moving from neuronal to human level, Teilhard forecasts the connecting up of a network of individual consciousness via "a direct tuning":

> In nascent super-humanity... the thousands of millions of single-minded individuals function in a nuclear way, by a direct tuning and resonance of their consciousness.[275]

At the close of "Centrology," Teilhard sets forth his "Corollaries and Conclusions." He begins by summarizing the evolution of consciousness in a sequence of five stages, and defining five points on the arc of centro-complexity at which occur categorically distinct evolutionary changes of state:

1. The appearance of life through association of fragments of centres.

2. The deepening of phyletic centres.

3. The emergence of reflective centres.

4. The birth of mankind (and reflective thought).

5. The dawn of Omega.[276]

In each of these five steps can be seen the effect of an increase in union, the creative energy of union causing changes of state—not simply due to some rearrangement or summation of parts, but, as Teilhard says, "under the influence of the radiation of Omega."[277] The holoflux theory analog of Teilhard's "radiation," of course, is Bohm's quantum potential function, "Q," radiating from the implicate order to emerge within space–time. Teilhard's "Omega point" can thus be viewed as a spherical portal, an analog of Bohm's "implicate order."[278]

In discussing the transition from Stage 4 to Stage 5, the change of state from the "birth of thought" to the "dawn of Omega," Teilhard insists that there should be *no* concern that such a change of state would mean a loss of personality or a death of our uniquely distinct egos; on the contrary, says Teilhard, the noosphere is comprised of an effective *re-union* of all individual "savable elements" of each personality. Even more, it serves to effect an even higher, more complete integration of *each* individual experience—a heightening of individual personality, "a cosmic personalization, the fruit of centrogenesis."[279] It is, stresses Teilhard, through each sub personality center-to-center contact *within* the noosphere (through the centre), that each individual personality is "super-personalized."[280] This center-to-center contact, Teilhard tells us, is a perceptual condition of each individual center merging into the noosphere; it *is not an epiphenomenon* of such a union, but a *requirement* for reaching full integral personalization:

> Something (someone) exists, in which each element gradually finds, by reunion with the whole, the completion of all the savable elements that have been formed in its individuality; thus the interior equilibrium of what we have called the Noosphere requires the presence *perceived by individuals* of a higher polar centre that directs, sustains and assembles the whole sheaf of our efforts.[281]

This process can be seen as a cybernetic feedback loop: the "higher polar centre" receives input from all of the "savable elements" of each "individuality," and working with this information the higher personality ("polar center") "sustains and assembles the whole sheaf of our efforts." In this way evolution proceeds through a continuous cyclic process of individual centres developing in space–time, merging into their respective centres through the directional "drift" of centro-complexity, *but not being lost* in the merger.

> To the extent that the grain of consciousness is *personalized*, it becomes released from its material support in the phylum ... detached from the matrix of complexity, and meets the ultimate pole of all convergence.[282]

Finally, the fifth stage in the process of centro-complexity, "the dawn of Omega," occurs at the point where *thought* transforms into omni-contact with all other centres, as well as with the "higher" (n + 1) center of personality, at which point there is a flaring forth into a categorically new mode of reflective consciousness, effecting a major change in state. Teilhard concludes that "far from tending to be confused together, the reflective centres intensify their *ego* the more they concentrate together."[283]

Isospheres

A key concept developed in "Centrology" is Teilhard's model of "isospheres," which he defines as "surfaces of equal centro-complexity."[284] He sees evolution catalyzed on these isospheres when "a maximum density of particles with a corresponding maximum of tentative gropings is produced on each isosphere." Listed in Table 3 are "isospheres" that have been defined for planet Earth, arranged in radial order.

These various regions of the planet each have their own unique and identifiable physical characteristics (temperature, density, etc.), and each might be considered an isosphere of the planet.

Table 3

Isospheres of Planet Earth

Scientific designation	Above/below sea level (miles)
Exosphere	310–620 mi.
Ionosphere or Plasmasphere	37–271 mi.
Thermosphere	56–311 mi.
Mesosphere	31–53 mi.
Stratosphere	10–30 mi.
Troposphere	4–12 mi.
Hydrosphere	0 to -5 mi.
Lithosphere or "rocky crust" (upper layer, crustal rocks) (0°–870° C.)	-275 mi.

Mantle (870°–3700° C)
    Upper Mantle (870° C)
    Asthenosphere (100–250 km deep)
Inner Mantle (semi rigid, 870°–3700° C)
	-21 to -1793 mi.

Outer Core (molten, 3700°–5000° C, 1370 miles thick)	-1800 mi.
Inner Core (Crystalline iron/nickel) (5000°–7200° C, 750-mile sphere)	-2170 mi.

Note. Data adapted from Tarbuck and Lutgens, *Earth Science*, 6-71.

Teilhard's use of the word "isosphere" is focused less upon the physics of geology and more upon the physics of metaphysics—a topology of consciousness, as he states in "Centrology":

> Thus there emerges the pattern of a *centred universe*—elements of equal complexity (and hence

of equal centricity) being spread out over what we may call isospheres of consciousness.[285]

Fig. 11 depicts a topological model of nested isospheres surrounding Teilhard's Omega. According to Teilhard, these isospheres of consciousness are concentric, "the radius of each sphere diminishing as the complexity increases."[286]

Isospheres

Planck holosphere
(diameter 10^{-35} meters)

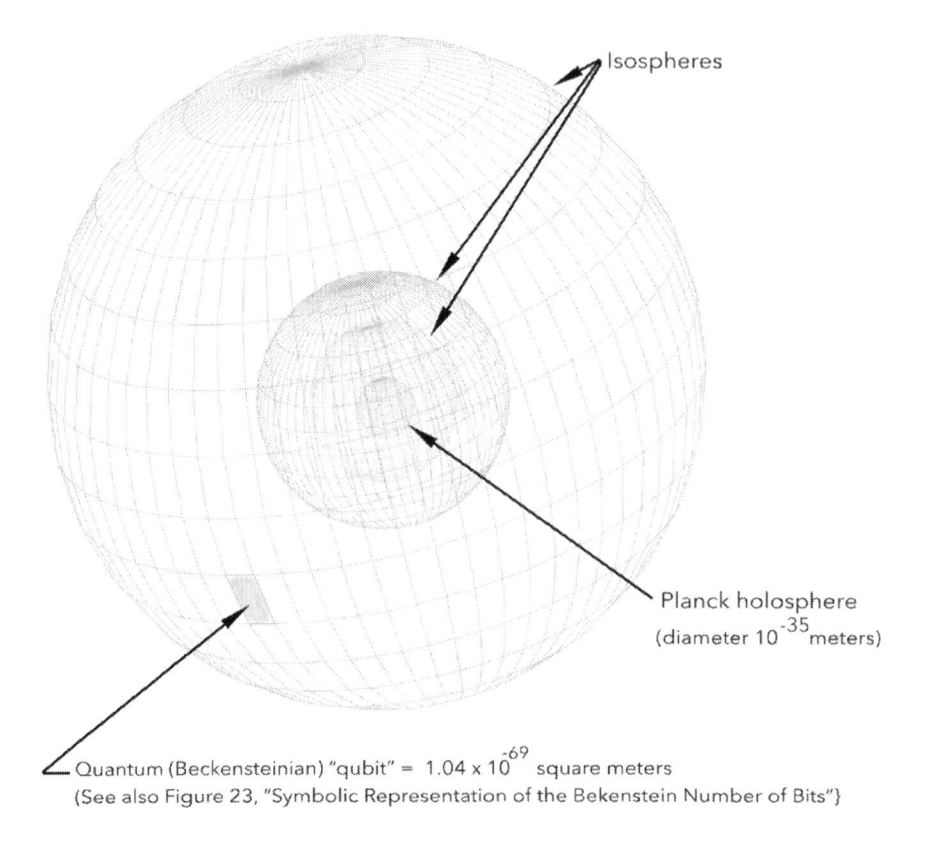

Quantum (Beckensteinian) "qubit" = 1.04×10^{-69} square meters
(See also Figure 23, "Symbolic Representation of the Bekenstein Number of Bits")

Figure 11. Isospheres surrounding Planck holosphere.

Here, Teilhard has clearly indicated the direction in which he sees increased consciousness: toward the centre, in the direction of Omega. According to quantum theory, the radial distance between any two nested isospheres may be no less than the Planck length (the smallest possible dimension of space), and this leads us to visualize an enormous yet finite series of isospheres in space–time, nested like Russian dolls or perhaps like separate capacitor plates in in an electronic circuit, beginning at the boundary of the Planck holosphere (enclosing Omega, the implicate order) and reaching an outer limit at the current (continuously expanding) diameter of the universe.

In this cosmological topology of nested three-dimensional isospheres, electrons would not travel in planar, two-dimensional, circular orbits as depicted in Bohr's model, but are "smeared out" as holonomic patterns of tangential flux over the surface boundaries of three-dimensional shells covering the surface areas of the isosphere.[287]

As we move outward from the central Planck holosphere into isospheres of higher radial dimensions, each holosphere must be separated, minimally, by one Planck length. The manifestation of these isospheres in space–time would provide the geometric capacity for storing multiple qubits of information, as previously developed by John Wheeler in considering the event horizon of a black hole. Thus, we may envision quantum states in a series of holospheric shells extending from the central Planck holosphere to the current boundary of the universe as spheres rather than rings. The universe here can be seen to consist of an almost infinite holoplenum of intersecting concentric shells of implicate order holospheres throughout space–time.

As seen in Bohr's model, for an electron cannot move from one shell to another shell *continuously* through some intervening space–time gap; instead, it is seen to execute a quantum leap to the adjacent level, transitioning from one isospheric shell to another during a single Planck time cycle at the rate of 5×10^{-44} seconds. The energy formations appear at the next holosphere shell at the "clock-speed" of light—not moving linearly within space–time as normally understood, but moving alternately between explicate spacetime and implicate nondual domains of being, nudging every centre toward an ever-so-slightly new direction within their evolutionary arcs in space–time.

Such a transformation might also be identified with Jean Gebser's "mutation of consciousness," the evolutionary mutation into what Gebser calls "integral consciousness."[288] In full agreement with Teilhard's assertion that evolution precludes loss of experienced personality, Gebser assures us that in evolving structures of consciousness, previous properties and potentialities do indeed survive:

> In contrast to biological mutations, these mutations of consciousness do not assume or require the disappearance of previous potentialities and properties, which, in this case, are immediately integrated into the new structure.[289]

Like Gebser, Teilhard observes that all personalities are incomplete and continually evolving, however slowly, and compares our individual personalities to the fragments of centres that seek for one another in the pre-living zones of matter, reminding us that "at our level of evolution we are still no more than rough drafts."[290] Teilhard here states with emphasis, *"the personal—considered quantitatively no less than qualitatively—is continually on the upgrade in the universe."*[291]

It is clear that in his writings Pierre Teilhard de Chardin, the trained anthropologist, regarded his theories of hyperphysics not as philosophy or metaphysics, but as an extension of physical science. He argues for a convergence—not a union—of physics and metaphysics, and in a topological, geodesic-like metaphor, defends his hyperphysics as being distinct yet parallel to existing categories of inquiry:

> Just like meridians as they approach the pole, so science, philosophy, and religion necessarily converge in the vicinity of the whole. They converge, I repeat, but without merging, and never ceasing to attack the real from different angles and levels right to the end.... It is impossible to attempt a general scientific interpretation of the universe without *seeming* to intend to explain it right to the end. But only take a closer look at it, and you will see that this hyperphysics still is not metaphysics.[292]

Breaking Teilhard's "Death-Barrier"

One of Teilhard de Chardin's mature conclusions is that our entire consciousness is *not* snuffed out when our material bodies die. If consciousness manifests as energy, then following Einstein's observation that "energy cannot be created or destroyed, it can only be changed from one form to another," any signal composed of an energy of consciousness must follow the same pattern.[293] While there may be a transformation of energy, there can be no absolute destruction, because energy (specifically the modulated energy flux of a conscious entity) cannot suddenly vanish. Such a view is, simply, superstition.

"The Death-Barrier and Co-Reflection"

By the very logic of evolution, in order for the species to learn, adapt, and preserve experiences gathered in the space–time domain, evolution at the human stage must break the "Death-Barrier," a term Teilhard develops in one of his final essays, "The Death-Barrier and Co-Reflection," completed January 1, 1955, three months before his own death on Easter Sunday, April 10:

> When biological evolution has reached its *reflective* stage ("self-evolution") it can continue to function

only in so far as man comes to realize that there is some *prima facie* evidence that the death-barrier *can* be broken.[294]

Teilhard had written previously of his own participatory experiences supporting his belief in an immortality of consciousness in a letter to his paleontologist colleague and friend, Helmut de Terra:

> My visible actions and influence count for very little beside my secret self. My real treasure is, *par excellence*, that part of my being which the centre, where all the sublimated wealth of the universe converges, cannot allow to escape. The reality, which is the culminating point of the universe, can only develop in partnership with ourselves by keeping us within the supreme personality: we cannot help finding ourselves personally immortal.[295]

Teilhard assumes that if there is a part, or region, or mode, or domain of our consciousness that continues beyond our bodies, beyond the death of our bodies, as he says in "Breaking the Death-Barrier," then should we not then be motivated to know and even explore that domain? That is the real treasure he is sharing with us: once specific memories are gone, the personality lives on, "keeping us within the supreme personality," within the implicate order, at the center, everywhere. But this "personality of the transcendent" can be seen, by mystics at least, even before the approach of the Death-Barrier.[296]

Not only does Teilhard categorically reject the majority of contemporary humankind's tacit assumption that death is "the end" (i.e., the end of individual consciousness); he worries that such an erroneous stance might delay what he saw as the natural emergence of a noosphere, cultivated and powered by human conscious energy, a collective holonomic energy modulated by and powered by living homo sapiens.[297]

The Cross the Trinity and the Centric

In 1950 Teilhard describes his vision of the Cross, the Trinity, and the Centric. He begins by reiterating a recurrent theme in his writing, talking about the "two tendencies" between which there is a "heightening of the antagonism between the 'tangential' forces that make us dependent upon one another" and "the 'radial' aspirations that urge us towards attaining the incommunicable core of our own person."[298] These two tendencies, seen as vectors of the energies of consciousness standing at right angles to one another, form a cross, the intersection of which is our own center of homonized consciousness (Fig. 12).

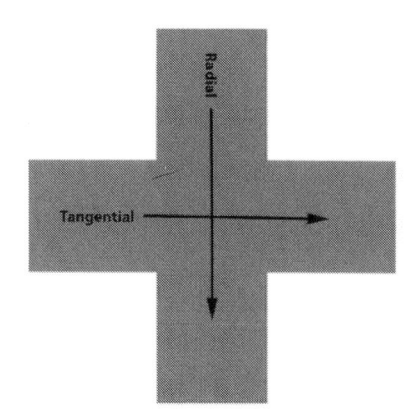

Figure 12. Teilhard's Cross: Tangential & Radial

This "heightening of antagonism" Teilhard describes can be seen clearly today in the seemingly abject polarity between the geo-political, corporate forces of the *tangential* as contrasted with the increasingly spiritualized *radial* forces of homonized liberal thinkers, altruists, mystics, and religious. It can be seen in the political polarization within our own government and in the polarization within countries across the world in recent years.

Teilhard would understand this polarization in the 21st century and say that under irresistible pressure, our planet "is contracting upon itself," and, accordingly, "we constantly feel, in ourselves and all around ourselves, a heightening of the antagonism between the 'tangential' forces that make us dependent upon one another, and the 'radial' aspirations."[299]

But in spite of these deeply felt antagonisms, Teilhard maintains a great reservoir of hope, based upon what he foresees as resolution in a spiral of complex centrification toward Omega, the Centric, the Christic (Fig. 13):

> Here we move into what is indeed a remarkable, an astonishing region where the Cosmic, the Human and the Christic meet and so open up a new domain, *the Centric*; and there the manifold oppositions which constitute the unhappiness and anxieties of our life begin to disappear.[300]

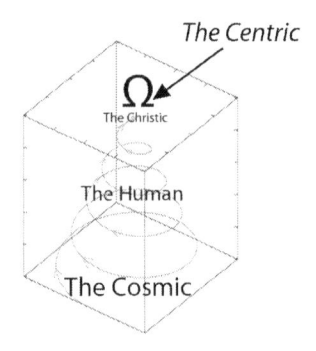

Figure 13. Teilhard's Spiral: The Cosmic, The Human, and The Christic.

The Noosphere, Omega, and The Christic

Thus, in the broad arc of the evolution (and homonization) of consciousness in the universe, Teilhard's final vision is a model that gives us a way of understanding how the forces of centro-complexification have led the energies of *The Cosmic*, after 14.6 billion years, into and through convergence into *The Human*, which is even now further centro-complexifying through the homonization of an isosphere, the Noosphere.

And at the center of this Noosphere, powered by The Centric (see Fig. 14), is *The Christic, the Omega,* and The Cosmic and The Human are inexorably being drawn toward its threshold.

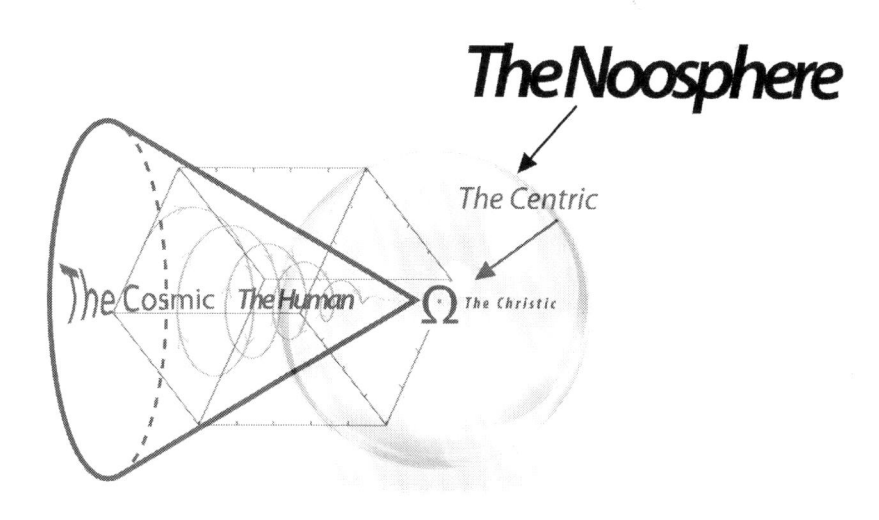

93

Figure 14. Noogenesis and the Noosphere.

At the age of sixty-five, while still in Peking, Teilhard writes "Suggestions for a New Theology," in which he affirms that religious thinking "cannot develop except traditionally, collectively, and 'phyletically.'"[301] Yet later in the same essay he suggests that if "we identify the cosmic Christ of faith with the Omega Point of science, then everything in our outlook is clarified and broadened, and falls into harmony."[302]

Omega Point of Science = *Cosmic Christ of Faith*

Here he has married (or grafted) his educationally derived scientific thinking with his phyletically derived religious thinking into a teleological identity. Having established this point of commonality, he ends his essay with the section "A New Mystical Orientation: The Love of Evolution," in which he discusses "the heart, with all that the word implies of vital and dynamic fullness." [303]

Now, having established the common mathematical point of convergence, Teilhard re-energizes the universe of cosmogenesis with the amorization of Christogenesis.

Cosmogeneis = *Christogenesis*

He says,"We now find that it is becoming not only possible but *imperative* literally to *love* evolution."[304]

It is through this amorization of a universe—and of a process that had previously grown cold through a sterilizing vision of science after Newton—that we will be able finally "to communicate, to 'super-communicate', with him through all the height, the breadth, the depths and the multiplicity of the organic powers of space and time."[305] Finally, on the last page of his essay, when summing up the "The Love of Evolution," Teilhard writes:

> Love, in consequence, is undoubtedly the single higher form towards which, as they are transformed, all the other sorts of spiritual energy converge—as one might expect in a universe built on the plane of union and by the forces of union.[306]

References

Abi-Talib. 2008. *Al-Saheefah Al-Alawiyah or The Alawite Book*. London: Forgotten Books.

Archibald, Douglas N. 2010. *The Story of Trinidad. Vol. I: The Age of Conquest, 1498–1623, Vol. II: The Age of Settlement 1624–1797*. Trinidad and Tobago: Aleong and Montgomery.

Sri Aurobindo Ghose. 1949. *The Life Divine*. 3rd ed. New York: India Library Society.

———. 1955. *The Synthesis of Yoga*. Pondicherry: Sri Aurobindo International University Centre.

———. 1972. *Hymns to the Mystic Fire*. Pondicherry: Sri Aurobindo Ashram.

———. 1972. *The Upanishads: Texts, Translations and Commentaries*. Pondicherry: Sri Aurobindo Ashram.

———. 1997. *Tales of Prison Life*. Pondicherry, India: Sri Aurobindo Ashram.

Bailey, Gregory. 2003. *The Study of Hinduism*. Columbia, SC: The University of South Carolina Press.

Barnhart, Bruno. 2001. "Christian Self-Understanding in the Light of the East." In *Purity of Heart and Contemplation: A Monastic Dialogue Between Christian and Asian Traditions*, 291–308. New York: Camaldolese Hermits of America, Inc.

Blofeld, John. 1972. *The Wheel of Life: The Autobiography of a Western Buddhist*. 2nd ed. Berkeley: Shambala.

Bohm, David. 1951. *Quantum Theory*. New York: Prentiss-Hall.

———. 1952. "A Suggested Interpretation of the Quantum Theory in Terms of 'Hidden Variables,' Vol. 1." *Physical Review* 85 (2): 166–93. Retrieved from http://fma.if.usp.br/~amsilva/Artigos/p166_1.pdf.

———. 1965. *The Special Theory of Relativity*. Philadelphia: John Benjamins.

———. 1978. "The Enfolding-Unfolding Universe: A Conversation with David Bohm." In *The Holographic Paradigm and Other Paradoxes: Exploring the Leading Edge of Science*, edited by Ken Wilber, 44–104. Boulder, CO: Shambhala.

———. 1979. *A Question of Physics: Conversations in Physics and Biology*, edited by P. Buckley and F. David Peat. London: Kegan Paul.

———. 1980. *Wholeness and the Implicate Order*. London: Routledge.

———. 1985. *Unfolding Meaning: A Weekend of Dialogue with David Bohm*. London: Routledge.

———. 1986. "The Implicate Order and the Super-Implicate Order." In *Dialogues with Scientists and Sages: The Search for Unity*, edited by Renée Weber, 23–49. New York: Routledge.

———. 1987. "Hidden Variables and the Implicate Order." In *Quantum Implications: Essays in Honour of David Bohm*, edited by B. J. Hiley and F. David Peat, 33–45. London: Routledge.

———. 1989. "Meaning and Information." In *The Search for Meaning: The New Spirit in Science and Philosophy*, edited by Paavo Pylkkänen, 43–85. Northamptonshire: The Aquarian Press.

———. 1990a. "Beyond Limits: A Full Conversation with David Bohm." Interview by Bill Angelos for Dutch public television. Posted March 5, 2011. Retrieved from http://bohmkrishnamurti.com/beyond-limits/

———. 1990b. "A New Theory of the Relationship of Mind and Matter." *Philosophical Psychology* 3 (2): 271–86.

Bohm, David, and Basil J. Hiley. 1993. *The Undivided Universe: An Ontological Interpretation of Quantum Theory*. London: Routledge.

Bohm, David, and J. Krishnamurti. 1985. *The Ending of Time: Where Philosophy and Physics Meet*. New York: Harper Collins.

Bohm, David, and J. Krishnamurti. 1999. *The Limits of Thought: Discussions between J. Krishnamurti and David Bohm*. London: Routledge.

Bohm, David, and F. David Peat. 1987. *Science, Order, and Creativity*. London: Routledge.

Bohm, David, and R. Weber. 1982. "Nature as Creativity." *ReVision* 5 (2): 35–40.

Booth, J. C., S. A. Koren, and Michael A. Persinger. 2005. "Increased Feelings of the Sensed Presence and Increased Geomagnetic Activity at the Time of the Experience During

Exposures to Transcerebral Weak Complex Magnetic Fields." *International Journal of Neuroscience* 115 (7): 1039–65.

Chaudhuri, Haridas. 1954. *The Philosophy of Integralism: The Metaphysical Synthesis in Sri Aurobindo's Teaching.* Pondicherry, India: Sri Aurobindo Ashram Trust.

Chaudhuri, Haridas. 1974. *Being, Evolution & Immortality: An Outline of Integral Philosophy.* Wheaton, Ill: A Quest Book.

Eliot, Thomas Stearns. 1943. *Four Quartets.* New York: Harcourt Brace.

Fourier, Jean-Baptiste. 1822. *The Analytical Theory of Heat.* English translation published 1878.

Fox, Matthew. 1988. *The Coming of the Cosmic Christ.* New York: Harper One.

Gebser, Jean. 1949. *The Ever-Present Origin: Part One: Foundations of the Aperspectival World.* Translated by J. Keckeis. Stuttgart, Germany: Deutsche Verlags-Anstalt.

Heehs, Peter. 2008. *The Lives of Sri Aurobindo.* New York: Columbia University Press.

James, William. 1950. *The Principles of Psychology*, 2 vols. New York: Dover.

———. (1909) 1998. *A Pluralistic Universe: Hibbert Lectures on the Present Situation in Philosophy.* New York: Longmans, Green, and Co.

Joye, Shelli R. 2016. *The Pribram–Bohm Holoflux Theory of Consciousness: An Integral*

Interpretation of the Theories of Karl Pribram, David Bohm, and Pierre Teilhard de Chardin (Doctoral dissertation). Available from ProQuest Dissertations and Theses database. (UMI No. 1803306323).

Jung, Carl G. 1968. "Psychology and Alchemy." In Vol. 12 of *The Collected Works of C. G. Jung*. Edited and translated by Gerald Adler and R. F. C. Hull. 2nd ed. Princeton, NJ: Princeton University.

———. (1946) 1969. "A Psychological Approach to the Dogma of the Trinity." In Vol. 11 of *The Collected Works of C. G. Jung*, translated by R. F. C. Hull, 159–234. 2nd ed. Princeton, NJ: Princeton University.

———. (1946) 1969. "On the Nature of the Psyche." In Vol. 8 of *The Collected Works of C. G. Jung*, translated by R. F. C. Hull, 159–234. 2nd ed. Princeton, NJ: Princeton University.

Keats, John. (1818) 2010. *Endymion: A Poetic Romance*. Whitefish, MT: Kessinger.

Kropf, Richard W. 2015. *Einstein and the Image of God: A Response to Contemporary Atheism*. Johannesberg, MI: Stellamar Publications.

Merrill-Wolf, Franklin. 1973. *The Philosophy of Consciousness Without an Object*. New York: Julian Press.

McKenna, Terence. 1993. *True Hallucinations: Being an Account of the Author's Extraordinary Adventures in the Devil's Paradise*. New York: HarperCollins.

Merton, Thomas. 1948. *The Seven Story Mountain*. New York: Harcourt.

Mishra, Rammurti. 1973. *The Yoga Sutras: Textbook of Yoga Psychology*. New York: Anchor Press.

Muller, Julius Eduard. 1880. "File:Tropenmuseum_Royal_Tropical_Institute_Objectnumber_60008905_Een_groep_Arowakken_en_Karaiben_in_fe.jpg" (graphic file). September 9, 2009. Wikimedia Commons. Retrieved from https://upload.wikimedia.org/wikipedia/commons/5/57/Tropenmuseum_Royal_Tropical_Institute_Objectnumber_60008905_Een_groep_Arowakken_en_Karaiben_in_fe.jpg

Ouspensky, P.D. 1949. *In Search of the Miraculous: Fragments of an Unknown Teaching*. New York: Harcourt.

Panikkar, Raimundo. 1973. *The Trinity and the Religious Experience of Man: Icon—Person—Mystery*. New York: Orbis Books.

———. 2010. *The Rhythm of Being: The Gifford Lectures*. New York: Orbis Books.

Radhakrishnan, Sarvepalli. 1957. *History of Philosophy Eastern and Western: Volume I*. London: George Allen & Unwin, Ltd.

———. 1971. *Indian Philosophy: Volume II*. London: George Allen & Unwin, Ltd.

Roy, Dilip Kumar. 1952. *Sri Aurobindo Came to Me*. Pondicherry: Sri Aurobindo Ashram Trust.

Spiegelberg, Frederic. 1951. *Spiritual Practices of India*. San Francisco: The Greenwood Press.

Stapledon, Olaf. 1968. *Last and First Men and Star Maker*. New York: Dover.

Teilhard de Chardin, Pierre. (1916) 1968. "Cosmic Life." In *Writings in Time of War*, translated by René Hague, 14–71. London: William Collins Sons.

———. (1916) 1978. "Christ in Matter." In *The Heart of Matter*, translated by René Hague, 61–67. New York: Harcourt Brace Jovanovich.

———. (1917) 1978. "Nostalgia for the Front." In *The Heart of Matter*, translated by René Hague, 168–81. New York: Harcourt Brace Jovanovich.

———. (1918a) 1978. "The Great Monad." In *The Heart of Matter*, translated by René Hague, 182–95. New York: Harcourt Brace Jovanovich.

———. (1918b) 1978. "My Universe." In *The Heart of Matter*, translated by René Hague, 196–208. New York: Harcourt Brace Jovanovich. ———. (1923) 1966. "Hominization." In The Vision of the Past, translated by J. M. Cohen, 51–79. New York: Harper & Row.

———. (1931) 1969. "The Spirit of the Earth." In *Human Energy*, translated by J. M. Cohen, 93–112. New York: Harcourt Brace Jovanovitch.

———. (1937) 1969. "The Phenomenon of Spirituality." In *Human Energy*, translated by J. M. Cohen, 93–112. New York: Harcourt Brace Jovanovitch.

———. (1941) 1976. "The Atomism of Spirit." In *Activation of Energy*, translated by René Hague, 21–57. London: William Collins Sons.

———. (1942) 1976. "Man's Place in the Universe." In *The Vision of the Past*, translated by J.M. Cohen, 216–33. New York: Harper & Row.

———. (1943) 1969. "Human Energy." In *Human Energy*, translated by J. M. Cohen, 113–62. New York: Harcourt Brace Jovanovitch.

———. (1944) 1976. "Centrology: An Essay in a Dialectic of Union." In *Activation of Energy*, translated by René Hague, 97–127. London: William Collins Sons.

———. (1945) 1959. "Life and the Planets." In *The Future of Man*, translated by Norman Denny, 97–123. New York: Harper & Row.

———. (1946) 1976. "Outline of a Dialectic of Spirit." In *Activation of Energy*, translated by René Hague, 143–51. London: William Collins Sons.

———. (1948) 1975. "My Fundamental Vision." In *Toward the Future*, translated by René Hague, 163–208. London: William Collins Sons.

———. (1949) 1956. "The Formation of the Noosphere II." In *Man's Place in Nature: The Human Zoological Group*, translated by René Hague, 96–121. New York: Harper & Row.

———. (1950a) 1978. "The Heart of Matter." In *The Heart of Matter*, translated by René Hague, 15–79. New York: Harcourt Brace Jovanovich.

———. (1950b) 1976. "The Zest for Living." In *Activation of Energy*, translated by René Hague, 229–43. London: William Collins Sons.

———. (1951a) 1976. "The Convergence of the Universe." In *Activation of Energy*, translated by René Hague, 281–96. London: William Collins Sons.

———. (1951b) 1976. "A Mental Threshold Across Our Path: From Cosmos to Cosmogenesis." In *Activation of Energy*, translated by René Hague, 251–68. London: William Collins Sons.

———. (1951c) 1975. "Some Notes on the Mystical Sense: An Attempt at Clarification" In *Toward the Future*, translated by René Hague, 209–11. London: William Collins Sons.

———. (1953a) 1976. "The Activation of Human Energy." In *Activation of Energy*, translated by René Hague, 359–93. London: William Collins Sons.

———. (1953b) 1976. "The Energy of Evolution." In *Activation of Energy*, translated by René Hague, 359–72. London: William Collins Sons.

———. (1953c) 1976. "The Stuff of the Universe." In *Activation of Energy*, translated by René Hague, 375–83. London: William Collins Sons.

———. (1953d) 1976. "Universalization and Union." In *Activation of Energy*, translated by René Hague, 77–95. London: William Collins Sons.

———. (1954) 1956. "The Nature of the Point Omega." In *The Appearance of Man*, translated by J.M. Cohen, 271–73. New York: Harper & Row.

———. (1955) 1976. "The Death-Barrier and Co-Reflection, or the Imminent Awakening of Human Consciousness to the Sense of Its Irreversibility." In *Activation of Energy*, translated by René Hague, 395–406. London: William Collins Sons.

———. 1956. *The Appearance of Man*. Translated by J. M. Cohen. New York: Harper & Row.

———. 1959. *The Phenomenon of Man*. Translated by Bernard Wall. New York: Harper & Row.

———. 1960. *The Divine Milieu*. New York: Harper & Row.

———. 1961. *The Making of a Mind: Letters from a Soldier–Priest 1914–1919*. Translated by Rene Hague. New York: Harper & Row.

———. 1962. *Letters from a Traveler*. New York: Harper & Row.

———. 1964. *The Phenomenon of Man*. New York: Harper & Row.

———. 1965. *Building the Earth*. Translated by Noël Lindsay. Wilkes-Barre, PA: Dimension Books.

———. 1968. *Letters to Two Friends 1926–1952*. New York: New American Library.

———. 1969a. *Human Energy*. Translated by J. M. Cohen. New York: Harcourt Brace Jovanovitch.

———. 1969b. *Letters to Leontine Zanta*. Translated by Bernard Wall. New York: Harper & Row.

———. 1971a. *Christianity and Evolution: Reflections on Science and Religion*. Translated by René Hague. London: William Collins Sons.

———. 1971b. *Pierre Teilhard de Chardin: L'Oeuvre Scientifique*. Edited by Nicole and Karl Schmitz-Moormann. 10 vols. Munich: Walter-Verlag.

———. 1972. *Lettres Intimes de Teilhard de Chardin a Auguste Valensin, Bruno de Solages, et Henri de Lubac 1919–1955*. Paris: Aubier Montaigne.

———. 1976. *Activation of Energy*. Translated by Rene Hague. London: William Collins Sons.

———. 1978. *The Heart of Matter*. Translated by René Hague. New York: Harcourt Brace Jovanovich.

———. 2003. *The Human Phenomenon*. Translated and edited by Sarah Appleton-Weber. Portland, OR: Sussex Academic. First published 1955.

Tiller, William. 2007. *Psychoenergetic Science*. Los Angeles: Pavior.

Whicher, Ian. 1998. *The Integrity of the Yoga Darsana: A Reconsideration of Classical Yoga*. New York: State University of New York Press.

Wilber, Ken. 1977. *The Spectrum of Consciousness*. Wheaton, IL: Theosophical Publishing House.

———. 1996. *A Brief History of Everything*. Boston, MA: Shambhala.

Yau, Shing-Tung, and Steve Nadis. 2010. *The Shape of Inner Space: String Theory and the Geometry of the Universe's Hidden Dimensions*. New York: Basic Books.

Index

A
Aurobindo, 97, 100, 102

B
Bergson, Henri, 7, 20, 26
Bohm, David, 50, 98, 99, 101
Bohr, Niels, 87

C
Camaldolese, 97
Catholic, 6, 16, 21, 31, 32, 42, 46
Christianity, 25, 107

E
Einstein, Albert, 89, 101

F
Frequency Domain, 56

H
holoflux, 56, 57, 82, 86, 91
Holoflux, 54, 100

I
Implicate Order, 55, 56, 58, 63, 74, 78, 80, 82, 87, 90

K
Krishnamurti, J., 99

N
Nonduality, 74

O
Noosphere, 16, 18, 25, 26, 28, 33, 34, 35, 36, 38, 44, 61, 62, 63, 66, 71, 75, 76, 82, 83, 90, 104

O
Omega point, 18, 20, 62, 64, 71, 76, 80, 82

P
Planck Length, 86, 87
Planck Time, 87
Pondicherry, 97, 100, 102
Pribram, Karl, 100, 101

Q
quantum potential, 74, 80, 82

T
Teilhard de Chardin, 3, 4, 5, 25, 42, 58, 64, 88, 89, 101, 103, 107, 113
The Human Phenomenon, 3, 23, 41, 64, 107, 113

U
Upanishads, 97

V
Vernadsky, Vladimir, 26

W
Wheeler, John, 87

Endnotes

[1] Teilhard de Chardin, *The Activation of Energy* (London: William Collins Sons & Co Ltd., 1976), 383.

[2] Johnjoe McFadden, "Synchronous Firing and Its Influence on the Brain's Electromagnetic Field: Evidence for an Electromagnetic Field Theory of Consciousness." *Journal of Consciousness Studies*, vol. 9, no. 4 (2002): 23.

[3] Susan Pockett, *The Nature of Consciousness: A Hypothesis* (Lincoln, NE: Writers Club Press, 2000), 7.

[4] In this text, I refer to him as Teilhard de Chardin, or simply Teilhard.

[5] Teilhard, *The Human Phenomenon*, 2.

[6] de Lubac, *The Religion of Teilhard de Chardin*; Henri de Lubac, eventually Cardinal de Lubac, was a Jesuit friend and correspondent of Teilhard's for more than 30 years.

[7] Teilhard, *Lettres Intimes*, 269.

[8] Teilhard, *The Phenomenon of Man*, xix.

[9] Teilhard, *L'oeuvre Scientifique*.

[10] B. Cheney, "Has Teilhard de Chardin 'Really' Joined the Within and the Without of Things?," 217.

[11] Ibid.

[12] Teilhard, "The Stuff of the Universe," 383. Essay written in 1953.

[13] King, *Spirit of Fire: The Life and Vision of Teilhard de Chardin*, 1.

[14] Ibid., 4.

[15] Ibid.

[16] Aczel, *The Jesuit and the Skull*, 72.

[17] Ibid., 24.

[18] Teilhard, *The Heart of Matter*, 25.

[19] Ibid., 74.

[20] Raven, *Teilhard de Chardin: Scientist and Seer*, 164–65.

[21] Bergson, *Creative Evolution*.

[22] Teilhard, *The Human Phenomenon*, 149.

[23] Teilhard, *The Heart of Matter*, 25.

[24] Teilhard, *Letters to Leontine Zanta*, 102.

[25] King, *Spirit of Fire*, 38.

[26] King, *Spirit of Fire*, 47.

[27] Ibid., 49.

[28] King, *Pierre Teilhard de Chardin*, 52; *Sidi Marabout*: An Arabic title of great esteem and honor; *Sidi* refers to a North African settled in France; *Marabout* designates a saint and ascetic blessed with divine favor.

[29] Aczel, *The Jesuit and the Skull*, 82.

[30] Ibid.

[31] Ibid., 77.

[32] Corte, *Pierre Teilhard de Chardin*, 15.

[33] Teilhard, "The Making of a Mind: Letters from a Soldier–Priest 1914–1919," 205.

[34] Teilhard, "Nostalgia for the Front," 172.

[35] Ibid.

[36] Horne, *The Price of Glory: Verdun 1916*, 328.

[37] Teilhard, "Christ in Matter," 61. Essay written in 1916.

[38] Tudzynski, Correia, and Keller. 2001. "Biotechnology and Genetics of Ergot Alkaloids."

[39] Teilhard, "Christ in Matter," 61–65. Essay written 1916.

[40] Teilhard, "The Christic," 83. Essay written in 1955.

41 Ibid.

42 Ibid., 82–83. Italic emphasis added.

43 King, *Spirit of Fire*, 59.

44 Ibid., 116.

45 Teilhard, "Human Energy," 118. Essay written in 1937.

46 Teilhard, "My Universe" 197. Essay written 14 April, 1918.

47 Teilhard, *The Divine Milieu*, 76–77.

48 Aczel, *The Jesuit and the Skull*, 123–24.

49 Ibid., 124.

50

51 Ibid., 132.

52 Ibid.

53 Association for Asian Studies, Southeast Conference, *Annals, Volumes 1–5*, 51.

54 King, *Spirit of Fire*, 233–34.

55 Teilhard, "Some Notes on the Mystical Sense: An Attempt at Clarification," 209. Essay written in 1951.

56 Teilhard, *The Human Phenomenon*, 2.

57 Teilhard, "Life and the Planets," 123. Lecture delivered in 1945

58 Ibid., 122.

59 Teilhard, "My Fundamental Vision," 164. Essay written in 1948.

60 Ibid., 83. Note that the Eocene Epoch lasted from 56 to 33.9 million years ago.

61 Ibid., 84.

62 Morgan, *Emergent Evolution: Gifford Lectures, 1921–22*.

63 Haisch, *The Purpose-Guided Universe: Believing in Einstein, Darwin, and God.*

64 King, *Spirit of Fire*, 233–34.

65 Ibid.

66 Leroy, "Teilhard de Chardin: The Man," 32.

67 Teilhard, *Letters from a Traveller*, 291

68 Teilhard, "The Zest for Living," 231.

69 King, *Pierre Teilhard de Chardin*, 17.

70 Teilhard, "Centrology: An Essay in the Dialectic of Union," written in 1944.

71 King, *Spirit of Fire*, 213.

72 Teilhard, "The Energy of Evolution," 361–62. Essay written in 1953.

73 Teilhard, "The Activation of Human Energy," 393. Essay written in 1953.

74 Teilhard, *Activation of Energy.*

75 Teilhard, "The Atomism of Spirit," 29. Essay written in 1941.

76 Teilhard, *The Human Phenomenon*, 109.

77 Teilhard, "The Zest for Living," 242. Essay written in 1950.

78 Ibid.

79 Teilhard, "The Activation of Human Energy," 393. Essay written in 1953.

80 Teilhard, footnote 10, "Centrology: An Essay in a Dialectic of Union," 121. Essay written in 1944.

81 Ibid., 120.

82 Teilhard, *Christianity and Evolution*, 56; and *The Appearance of Man*, 33.

[83] "Over and above the biosphere there is a *noosphere*."; Teilhard, *The Human Phenomenon*, 124.

[84] Samson and Pitt, *The Biosphere and Noosphere Reader*, 3.

[85] Teilhard, "The Great Monad," 182. Essay written in 1918.

[86] Teilhard, *The Heart of Matter*.

[87] Noosphere: from the Greek νοῦς (*nous*: "sense, mind, wit") and σφαῖρα (*sphaira*: "sphere, orb, globe"); Samson and Pitt, *The Biosphere and Noosphere Reader*.

[88] King, *Spirit of Fire*, 84.

[89] Speaight, *The Life of Teilhard de Chardin*, 117.

[90] Teilhard, as quoted in Cuénot, *Teilhard de Chardin: A Biographical Study*, 59.

[91] King, *Spirit of Fire*, 84.

[92] Bailes, *Science and Russian Culture in an Age of Revolutions*; the term "biosphere" had been in use since as early as 1900, popularized by the Austrian geologist Eduard Suess.

[93] Samson and Pitt, *The Biosphere and Noosphere Reader*, 94–95.

[94] Vernadsky, *The Biosphere*, 16.

[95] Aczel, *The Jesuit and the Skull*, 86.

[96] Teilhard, "Hominization," 61. Essay written in 1923.

[97] Ibid., 62.

[98] Ibid., 73–78.

[99] Teilhard, "The Death-Barrier and Co-Reflection," 402. Essay written in 1955.

[100] Ibid., 78.

[101] Teilhard., 25.

[102] Ibid, 24.

[103] Teilhard, *The Divine Milieu*, (New York: Harper & Row, 1960).

[104] Ibid., 128-129.

[105] Teilhard, *The Divine Milieu*, (New York: Harper & Row, 1960), 120.

[106] Teilhard, *Christianity and Evolution*, (London: William Collins Sons & Col Ltd., 1969), 160.

[107] Teilhard, *The Divine Milieu*, 128.

[108] Ibid., 180.

[109] Teilhard, "The Christic," in <u>The Heart of Matter</u>, translated by Rene Hague (Florida: Harcourt Brace Jovanovitch, 1976).

[110] Ibid., 82.

[111] Ibid., 90.

[112] King, *Spirit of Fire*, 104.

[113] Speaight, *The Life of Teilhard de Chardin*, 135.

[114] Radhakrishnan, *History of Philosophy Eastern and Western*, 57.

[115] Skrbina, *Panpsychism in the West*, 30.

[116] MacKenna, *Plotinus: The Enneads*.

[117] Radhakrishnan, *History of Philosophy Eastern and Western*, 115.

[118] MacKenna, *Plotinus: The Enneads*, 712.

[119] Jung, *Psychology and Alchemy*.

[120] Teilhard, "Centrology: An Essay in a Dialectic of Union," 127. Essay written in 1944.

[121] Teilhard, as quoted in Cuénot, *Teilhard de Chardin: A Biographical Study*, 59.

[122] Teilhard, "The Convergence of the Universe," 285. Essay written in 1951.

[123] Samson and Pitt, *The Biosphere and Noosphere Reader*, xi.

[124] Ibid., 2–3.

[125] Allaby and Allaby, *A Dictionary of Earth Science*, 72.

[126] A brane is a geometrical boundary of higher dimensional dimensions spaces. This concept is used in contemporary superstring theory and M-theory; see Susskind, *The Black Hole War*.

[127] Malinski, *Chemistry of the Heart*, 61.

[128] Radio Ukraine; Berg, *Broadcasting on the Short Waves, 1945 to Today*, 43.

[129] Walker, *Three Mile Island: A Nuclear Crisis in Historical Perspective*, 12.

[130] The data in this chart was recorded from the Geostationary Operational Environmental Satellites 8 and 10, weather satellites in geosynchronous orbit over the east and west coasts of the United States in the days before, during, and after the September 11, 2001, terrorist attacks.

[131] McCraty, Deyhle, and Childre, "The Global Coherence Initiative: Creating a Coherent Planetary Standing Wave," 75.

[132] McCraty, Deyhle, and Childre, "The Global Coherence Initiative: Creating a Coherent Planetary Standing Wave," 76.

[133] Teilhard, *Christianity and Evolution: Reflections on Science and Religion*, 231.

[134] King, *Spirit of Fire*, 97.

[135] Ibid., 98.

[136] Ibid., 106.

[137] Ibid., 106–8.

[138] Teilhard, "Letters to Two Friends 1926–1952," 5.

[139] Aczel, *The Jesuit and the Skull*, 78.

[140] Ibid.

[141] Ibid., 79.

[142] King, *Spirit of Fire*, 93.

[143] Cuénot, *Teilhard de Chardin: A Biographical Study*, 257.

[144] Ibid., 258.

[145] Leckie, *Delivered from Evil: The Saga of World War II*.

[146] Aczel, *The Jesuit and the Skull*, 213.

[147] King, *Spirit of Fire*, 230.

[148] Aczel, *The Jesuit and the Skull*, 221.

[149] King, *Spirit of Fire*, 230.

[150] Aczel, *The Jesuit and the Skull*,

[151] Ibid., 231.

[152] Dunwell, *The Hudson: America's River*, 140.

[153] Teilhard, "The Spirit of the Earth," 42. Essay written in 1931.

[154] Teilhard, "The Phenomenon of Spirituality," 96–97. Essay written in 1937.

[155] Teilhard, "The Nature of the Point Omega," 160.

[156] Teilhard, "From Cosmos to Cosmogenesis," 257. Essay written in 1951.

[157] Teilhard, "Centrology: An Essay in a Dialectic of Union," 103. Essay written in 1944.

[158] Ibid., 106.

[159] Ibid., 104.

[160] King, *Spirit of Fire*, 164.

[161] Skrbina, *Panpsychism in the West*.

162 Teilhard, *Activation of Energy*.

163 Teilhard, "The Phenomenon of Spirituality," 112.

164 Teilhard, *Building the Earth*, 67.

165 Bohm, *Wholeness and the Implicate Order*.

166 Teilhard, "The Phenomenon of Spirituality," 93. Essay written in 1937.

167 Ibid.

168 Ibid.

169 Ibid., 93–94.

170 Ibid.

171 Teilhard, "Human Energy," 130–31.

172 Teilhard, "The Phenomenon of Spirituality," 99.

173 Ibid., 98.

174 Ibid.

175 Ibid., 101.

176 Teilhard's final essay, written shortly before his death in 1955, is entitled "The Death-Barrier and Co-Reflection, or the Imminent Awakening of Human Consciousness to the Sense of Its Irreversibility."

177 Teilhard, "The Phenomenon of Spirituality," 103.

178 Note that the British spelling "centre" is used here and throughout textual discussion in this chapter, not only because it is in accordance with the spelling found in all published translations of Teilhard's work into English, but more specifically because in the context of Teilhard's metaphysics, the word *centre* is used to designate a "center of consciousness," rather than used simply as an adjective or a location designator.

179 Teilhard, "The Phenomenon of Spirituality," 104.

180 Ibid., 106.

181 Ibid., 105.

182 Ibid., 106.

183 Ibid.

184 Ibid., 105.

185 Ibid, 107.

186 Ibid., 107–8.

187 Ibid., 108.

188 Ibid., 109–11.

189 Ibid.

190 Ibid.

191 Ibid., 99.

192 Ibid., 101.

193 Ibid., 103.

194 Joye, *The Pribram–Bohm Holoflux Theory of Consciousness.*

195 Ibid., 93–94.

196 Gao, *Dark Energy: From Einstein's Biggest Blunder to the Holographic Universe.*

197 Teilhard, "Human Energy." Essay written in 1937.

198 Ibid., 117.

199 Ibid., 118. Emphasis added by author.

200 Ibid., 128.

201 Ibid., 129–30.

202 Jung, "On the Nature of the Psyche," 207.

203 Teilhard, "The Spirit of the Earth," 35. Essay written 1931.

204 Ibid., 33.

205 Teilhard, "Human Energy," 130–31.

206 Ibid., 131.

[207] Ibid.

[208] Ibid., 138.

[209] Ibid., 141.

[210] Teilhard, "Cosmic Life," 15; Note that it is here, in Teilhard's earliest known essay, written at Dunkirk in April 1916, that Teilhard first speaks at length about the centres and the sphere: "We are the countless centres of one and the same sphere."

[211] Teilhard, *Human Energy*, 143.

[212] Ibid., 143–44.

[213] Ibid., 144.

[214] Ibid., 145.

[215] de Lubac, *The Religion of Teilhard de Chardin*, 123.

[216] Teilhard, "Life and the Planets." Speech of 1945 published as an essay in 1946.

[217] Ibid., 122.

[218] Teilhard, *The Human Phenomenon*, 191–93.

[219] Teilhard, "Human Energy," 138.

[220] Teilhard, "The Activation of Human Energy," 393.

[221] Teilhard, "The Nature of the Point Omega," 272–73.

[222] Teilhard, "Human Energy," 162.

[223] Teilhard, "Centrology," 99.

[224] Ibid., 100.

[225] Ibid., 101.

[226] Ibid., 102.

[227] Ibid., 102, n1.

[228] Ibid. 102.

[229] Ibid., 103.

[230] Teilhard, "Man's Place in the Universe," 226. Essay written in 1942.

[231] Ibid., 226.

[232] Calculated by Drew Weisenberger, a detector scientist at the Department of Energy's Thomas Jefferson National Accelerator Facility. See Weisenberger, "Jefferson Lab Questions and Answers," para. 2.

[233] Teilhard, "The Atomism of Spirit," 40.

[234] Teilhard, *The Human Phenomenon*, 110.

[235] Teilhard, "Centrology," 103.

[236] Teilhard, "Universalization and Union," 91. Essay written in 1953.

[237] Teilhard, "Centrology," 120.

[238] Ibid., 110.

[239] Ibid.

[240] Teilhard, "Outline of a Dialectic of Spirit," 144.

[241] Teilhard, "Centrology," 103.

[242] Rescher, *G. W. Leibniz's Monadology*.

[243] Teilhard, "Centrology," 104.

[244] Ibid., 100.

[245] Ibid., 105.

[246] Ibid., 106.

[247] Ibid., 107.

[248] Ibid., 108.

[249] Ibid., 109.

[250] Sheldrake, *A New Science of Life: The Hypothesis of Morphic Resonance*.

[251] Teilhard, "Centrology," 109.

[252] Ibid.

[253] Ibid.

[254] Ibid., 110.

[255] Ibid.

[256] Ibid., 110–11.

[257] Ibid., 111.

[258] Ibid.

[259] Teilhard, "The Phenomenon of Spirituality," 100.

[260] Ibid., 99.

[261] Teilhard, *The Phenomenon of Man*, 73–74.

[262] Teilhard, "Centrology," 112.

[263] Ibid.

[264] Ibid.

[265] Ibid., 113.

[266] Ibid.

[267] Ibid.

[268] Assistance with these Latin translations was provided by Fr. Thomas Matus, PhD, a Camaldolese Benedictine monk, in an e-mail message to author, August 27, 2015.

[269] Teilhard, "Centrology," 114.

[270] Ibid.

[271] Ibid.

[272] Ibid.

[273] Teilhard, "The Formation of the Noosphere II," 111. Essay written in 1949.

[274] Booth, Koren, and Persinger, "Increased Feelings of the Sensed Presence During Exposures to Weak Magnetic Fields."

[275] Teilhard, "Centrology," 114–15.

[276] Ibid., 116.

277 Ibid., 115.

278 Joye, *The Pribram–Bohm Holoflux Theory of Consciousness*.

279 Ibid., 119.

280 Ibid., 116.

281 Teilhard, "Hominization," in *The Vision of the Past*, 78.

282 Teilhard, "Centrology," 122.

283 Ibid., 116–17.

284 Ibid., 100.

285 Teilhard, "Centrology," 102.

286 Ibid.

287 Goswami, *The Visionary Window*.

288 Gebser, *The Ever-Present Origin*, 37.

289 Ibid., 39.

290 Teilhard, "Centrology," 117.

291 Ibid.

292 Teilhard, *Human Phenomenon*, 2.

293 Einstein, *Autobiographical Notes*, 17.

294 Teilhard, "The Death-Barrier and Co-Reflection," 403.

295 de Terra, *Memories of Teilhard de Chardin*, 42.

296 Teilhard, "The Death-Barrier and Co-Reflection," 402.

297 Ibid., 403.

298 Teilhard. "The Divine Milieu" in <u>The Heart of Matter</u>. (New York: Harcourt Brace Jovanovich, Inc., 1978), 49–50.

299 Ibid., 50.

300 Teilhard, *The Heart of Matter*, 49.

301 Teilhard, *Christianity and Evolution*, 173–74.

[302] Ibid., 180.
[303]
[304] Ibid., 184.
[305] Ibid., 185.
[306] Ibid., 186.

Printed in Great Britain
by Amazon